THE
AZTECS

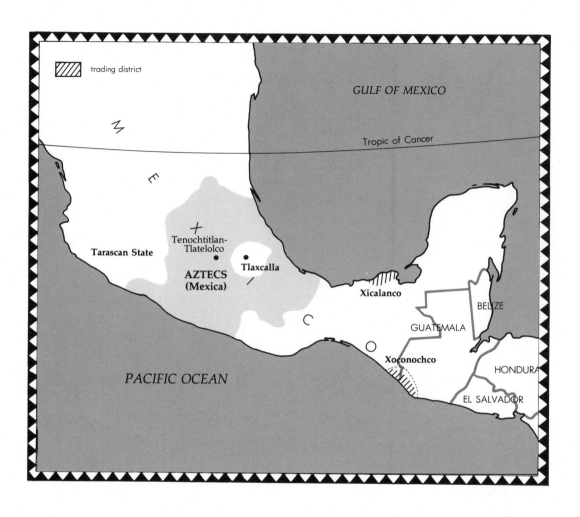

INDIANS OF NORTH AMERICA

THE
AZTECS

Frances F. Berdan
California State University, San Bernardino

Frank W. Porter III
General Editor

CHELSEA HOUSE PUBLISHERS
New York   Philadelphia

On the cover Mixtec-Aztec mask of wood covered with turquoise mosaic; inset eyes and teeth made of shell.

Chelsea House Publishers
Editor-in-Chief Nancy Toff
Executive Editor Remmel T. Nunn
Managing Editor Karyn Gullen Browne
Copy Chief Juliann Barbato
Picture Editor Adrian G. Allen
Art Director Maria Epes
Manufacturing Manager Gerald Levine

Indians of North America
Senior Editor Marjorie P. K. Weiser

Staff for **THE AZTECS**
Associate Editor Andrea E. Reynolds
Copy Editors Terrance Dolan, Karen Hammonds
Deputy Copy Chief Ellen Scordato
Editorial Assistant Tara P. Deal
Assistant Art Director Laurie Jewell
Designer Ghila Krajzman
Picture Researcher Ann Levy
Production Coordinator Joseph Romano

3   5   7   9   8   6   4   2

Library of Congress Cataloging in Publication Data

Berdan, Frances.
The Aztecs / Frances F. Berdan.
    p.   cm.—(Indians of North America)
Bibliography: p.
Includes index.
Summary: Examines the culture, history, and changing fortunes of the Aztec Indians.
ISBN 1-55546-692-3
        0-7910-0354-X (pbk.)
1. Aztecs. [1. Aztecs. 2. Indians of Mexico.]
I. Title. II. Series: Indians of North America (Chelsea House
Publishers)   88-10077
F1219.73.B46   1989   CIP
972'.01—dc 19   AC

CONTENTS

INDIANS OF NORTH AMERICA

The Abenaki

American Indian
  Literature

The Apache

The Arapaho

The Archaeology
  of North America

The Aztecs

The Cahuilla

The Catawbas

The Cherokee

The Cheyenne

The Chickasaw

The Chinook

The Chipewyan

The Choctaw

The Chumash

The Coast Salish
  Peoples

The Comanche

The Creek

The Crow

The Eskimo

Federal Indian Policy

The Hidatsa

The Huron

The Iroquois

The Kiowa

The Kwakiutl

The Lenape

The Lumbee

The Maya

The Menominee

The Modoc

The Montagnais-Naskapi

The Nanticoke

The Narragansett

The Navajo

The Nez Perce

The Ojibwa

The Osage

The Paiute

The Pima-Maricopa

The Potawatomi

The Powhatan Tribes

The Pueblo

The Quapaw

The Seminole

The Tarahumara

The Tunica-Biloxi

Urban Indians

The Wampanoag

Women in American
  Indian Society

The Yakima

The Yankton Sioux

The Yuma

CHELSEA HOUSE PUBLISHERS

INDIANS OF NORTH AMERICA: CONFLICT AND SURVIVAL

Frank W. Porter III

*The Indians survived our
open intention of wiping them
out, and since the tide turned
they have even weathered
our good intentions toward them,
which can be much more deadly.*

John Steinbeck
America and Americans

When Europeans first reached the North American continent, they found hundreds of tribes occupying a vast and rich country. The newcomers quickly recognized the wealth of natural resources. They were not, however, so quick or willing to recognize the spiritual, cultural, and intellectual riches of the people they called Indians.

The Indians of North America examines the problems that develop when people with different cultures come together. For American Indians, the consequences of their interaction with non-Indian people have been both productive and tragic. The Europeans believed they had "discovered" a "New World," but their religious bigotry, cultural bias, and materialistic world view kept them from appreciating and understanding the people who lived in it. All too often they attempted to change the way of life of the indigenous people. The Spanish conquistadores wanted the Indians as a source of labor. The Christian missionaries, many of whom were English, viewed them as potential converts. French traders and trappers used the Indians as a means to obtain pelts. As Francis Parkman, the 19th-century historian, stated, "Spanish civilization crushed the Indian; English civilization scorned and neglected him; French civilization embraced and cherished him."

Nearly 500 years later, many people think of American Indians as curious vestiges of a distant past, waging a futile war to survive in a Space Age society. Even today, our understanding of the history and culture of American Indians is too often derived from unsympathetic, culturally biased, and inaccurate reports. The American Indian, described and portrayed in thousands of movies, television programs, books, articles, and government studies, has either been raised to the status of the "noble savage" or disparaged as the "wild Indian" who resisted the westward expansion of the American frontier.

Where in this popular view are the real Indians, the human beings and communities whose ancestors can be traced back to ice-age hunters? Where are the creative and indomitable people whose sophisticated technologies used the natural resources to ensure their survival, whose military skill might even have prevented European settlement of North America if not for devastating epidemics and the disruption of the ecology? Where are the men and women who are today diligently struggling to assert their legal rights and express once again the value of their heritage?

The various Indian tribes of North America, like people everywhere, have a history that includes population expansion, adaptation to a range of regional environments, trade across wide networks, internal strife, and warfare. This was the reality. Europeans justified their conquests, however, by creating a mythical image of the New World and its native people. In this myth, the New World was a virgin land, waiting for the Europeans. The arrival of Christopher Columbus ended a timeless primitiveness for the original inhabitants.

Also part of this myth was the debate over the origins of the American Indians. Fantastic and diverse answers were proposed by the early explorers, missionaries, and settlers. Some thought that the Indians were descended from the Ten Lost Tribes of Israel, others that they were descended from inhabitants of the lost continent of Atlantis. One writer suggested that the Indians had reached North America in another Noah's ark.

A later myth, perpetrated by many historians, focused on the relentless persecution during the past five centuries until only a scattering of these "primitive" people remained to be herded onto reservations. This view fails to chronicle the overt and covert ways in which the Indians successfully coped with the intruders.

All of these myths presented one-sided interpretations that ignored the complexity of European and American events and policies. All left serious questions unanswered. What were the origins of the American Indians? Where did they come from? How and when did they get to the New World? What was their life—their culture—really like?

In the late 1800s, anthropologists and archaeologists in the Smithsonian Institution's newly created Bureau of American Ethnology in Washington, D. C., began to study scientifically the history and culture of the Indians of North America. They were motivated by an honest belief that the Indians were on the verge of extinction and that along with them would vanish their languages, religious beliefs, technology, myths, and legends. These men and women went out to visit, study, and record data from as many Indian communities as possible before this information was forever lost.

By this time there was a new myth in the national consciousness. American Indians existed as figures in the American past. They had performed a historical mission. They had challenged white settlers who trekked across the continent. Once conquered, however, they were supposed to accept graciously the way of life of their conquerors.

The reality again was different. American Indians resisted both actively and passively. They refused to lose their unique identity, to be assimilated into white society. Many whites viewed the Indians not only as members of a conquered nation but also as "inferior" and "unequal." The rights of the Indians could be expanded, contracted, or modified as the conquerors saw fit. In every generation, white society asked itself what to do with the American Indians. Their answers have resulted in the twists and turns of federal Indian policy.

There were two general approaches. One way was to raise the Indians to a "higher level" by "civilizing" them. Zealous missionaries considered it their Christian duty to elevate the Indian through conversion and scanty education. The other approach was to ignore the Indians until they disappeared under pressure from the ever-expanding white society. The myth of the "vanishing Indian" gave stronger support to the latter option, helping to justify the taking of the Indians' land.

Prior to the end of the 18th century, there was no national policy on Indians simply because the American nation had not yet come into existence. American Indians similarly did not possess a political or social unity with which to confront the various Europeans. They were not homogeneous. Rather, they were loosely formed bands and tribes, speaking nearly 300 languages and thousands of dialects. The collective identity felt by Indians today is a result of their common experiences of defeat and/or mistreatment at the hands of whites.

During the colonial period, the British crown did not have a coordinated policy toward the Indians of North America. Specific tribes (most notably the Iroquois and the Cherokee) became military and political pawns used by both the crown and the individual colonies. The success of the American Revolution brought no immediate change. When the United States acquired new territory from France and Mexico in the early 19th century, the federal government wanted to open this land to settlement by homesteaders. But the Indian tribes that lived on this land had signed treaties with European governments assuring their title to the land. Now the United States assumed legal responsibility for honoring these treaties.

At first, President Thomas Jefferson believed that the Louisiana Purchase contained sufficient land for both the Indians and the white population.

Within a generation, though, it became clear that the Indians would not be allowed to remain. In the 1830s the federal government began to coerce the eastern tribes to sign treaties agreeing to relinquish their ancestral land and move west of the Mississippi River. Whenever these negotiations failed, President Andrew Jackson used the military to remove the Indians. The southeastern tribes, promised food and transportation during their removal to the West, were instead forced to walk the "Trail of Tears." More than 4,000 men, women, and children died during this forced march. The "removal policy" was successful in opening the land to homesteaders, but it created enormous hardships for the Indians.

By 1871 most of the tribes in the United States had signed treaties ceding most or all of their ancestral land in exchange for reservations and welfare. The treaty terms were intended to bind both parties for all time. But in the General Allotment Act of 1887, the federal government changed its policy again. Now the goal was to make tribal members into individual landowners and farmers, encouraging their absorption into white society. This policy was advantageous to whites who were eager to acquire Indian land, but it proved disastrous for the Indians. One hundred thirty-eight million acres of reservation land were subdivided into tracts of 160, 80, or as little as 40 acres, and allotted to tribe members on an individual basis. Land owned in this way was said to have "trust status" and could not be sold. But the surplus land—all Indian land not allotted to individuals— was opened (for sale) to white settlers. Ultimately, more than 90 million acres of land were taken from the Indians by legal and illegal means.

The resulting loss of land was a catastrophe for the Indians. It was necessary to make it illegal for Indians to sell their land to non-Indians. The Indian Reorganization Act of 1934 officially ended the allotment period. Tribes that voted to accept the provisions of this act were reorganized, and an effort was made to purchase land within preexisting reservations to restore an adequate land base.

Ten years later, in 1944, federal Indian policy again shifted. Now the federal government wanted to get out of the "Indian business." In 1953 an act of Congress named specific tribes whose trust status was to be ended "at the earliest possible time." This new law enabled the United States to end unilaterally, whether the Indians wished it or not, the special status that protected the land in Indian tribal reservations. In the 1950s federal Indian policy was to transfer federal responsibility and jurisdiction to state governments, encourage the physical relocation of Indian peoples from reservations to urban areas, and hasten the termination, or extinction, of tribes.

Between 1954 and 1962 Congress passed specific laws authorizing the termination of more than 100 tribal groups. The stated purpose of the termination policy was to ensure the full and complete integration of Indians into American society. However, there is a less benign way to interpret this legislation. Even as termination was being discussed in Congress, 133 separate bills were introduced to permit the transfer of trust land ownership from Indians to non-Indians.

With the Johnson administration in the 1960s the federal government began to reject termination. In the 1970s yet another Indian policy emerged. Known as "self-determination," it favored keeping the protective role of the federal government while increasing tribal participation in, and control of, important areas of local government. In 1983 President Reagan, in a policy statement on Indian affairs, restated the unique "government to government" relationship of the United States with the Indians. However, federal programs since then have moved toward transferring Indian affairs to individual states, which have long desired to gain control of Indian land and resources.

As long as American Indians retain power, land, and resources that are coveted by the states and the federal government, there will continue to be a "clash of cultures," and the issues will be contested in the courts, Congress, the White House, and even in the international human rights community. To give all Americans a greater comprehension of the issues and conflicts involving American Indians today is a major goal of this series. These issues are not easily understood, nor can these conflicts be readily resolved. The study of North American Indian history and culture is a necessary and important step toward that comprehension. All Americans must learn the history of the relations between the Indians and the federal government, recognize the unique legal status of the Indians, and understand the heritage and cultures of the Indians of North America.

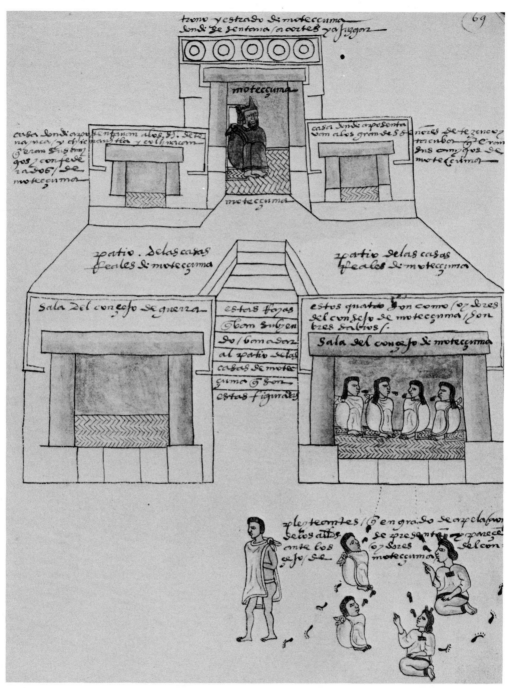

A page of the Codex Mendoza *(a manuscript written in picture symbols), showing Motecuhzoma's palace in Tenochtitlan. The two-story structure included council chambers and courtrooms. The ruler is seated inside on the second floor.*

MEXICO
AND THE
MEXICA

In November 1519, at the entrance to Tenochtitlan (Te-noch-TEE-tlan), one of the world's great cities, two men faced each other. Their encounter would ultimately change the world that each of them knew. Motecuhzoma Xocoyotzin (Mo-tek'w-SO-ma Sho-ko-YO-tseen) was the powerful emperor of many people and vast lands in Mexico. Hernando Cortés was the daring leader of a small band of troops recently arrived from Spain. Nearly half a century later, Bernal Díaz del Castillo, a soldier in Cortés's small army, recalled the moment:

> When Cortés saw, heard, and was told that the great Montezuma [Motecuhzoma] was approaching, he dismounted from his horse, and when he came near to Montezuma each bowed deeply to the other. Montezuma welcomed our Captain, and Cortés, speaking through Doña Marina, answered by wishing him very good health. Cortés, I think, offered Montezuma his right hand, but Montezuma refused it and extended his own. Then Cortés brought out a necklace. . . . This he hung round the great Montezuma's neck, and as he did so attempted to embrace him. But the great princes who stood round Montezuma grasped Cortés's arm to prevent him, for they considered this an indignity.

Díaz del Castillo was reporting not just the meeting of two leaders but the collision of two very different cultures. The meeting between Motecuhzoma and Cortés was soon followed by a series of battles that would decide who would rule Mexico, the Aztecs or the Spaniards. A long period of conflict and compromise followed. During this time the two cultures blended to form what would become the Mexico of today. There many Indians live, still speaking native languages, weaving cloth in the ancient manner, and growing and cooking food much as their Aztec ancestors did.

Aztec ruler Motecuhzoma and Hernando Cortés meet in Tenochtitlan, 1519. Doña Marina, Cortés's translator, stands behind him. The chairs are an invention of the artist. The deer, birds, and pile of maize are gifts from Motecuhzoma to Cortés.

The Spaniards who encountered the exotic Aztec civilization wrote volumes about their impressions of the people of central Mexico and their customs. One, known as the Anonymous Conqueror, described the people as "well proportioned, tending to be tall rather than short. They are swarthy, like leopards, of good manners and gestures. For the most part they are very skillful, robust and tireless, and at the same time the most moderate men known.

They are very warlike and face death fearlessly."

Another conqueror, Francisco de Aguilar, described his encounter with Aztec warriors:

Many of [the warriors] carried standards and gold shields, and other insignia which they wore strapped to their backs, giving them an appearance of great ferocity, since they also had their faces stained, and grimaced horribly, giving great leaps and shouts and cries. These put such fear into us that many of the Spaniards asked for confession.

Toribio de Benavente (also known as Motolinia), a 16th-century friar, saw another side: "Their understanding is keen, modest, and quiet, not proud or showy as in other nations." Alonso de Zorita, a 16th-century Spanish administrator, observed that "these people are by nature very long-suffering, and nothing will excite or anger them. They are very obedient and teachable. . . . The more noble they are, the more humility they display."

The early Spanish view of the Aztecs was of a people who were warlike yet moderate, ferocious yet mannerly. These views seem contradictory, but the Spaniards met the Aztecs only in limited circumstances. Although their impressions help us to understand the Aztecs, their views are neither complete nor unbiased. Aztec customs and behaviors do make sense in terms of their own view of their world. They saw their lives—including warfare, the passage of time, and even the corn plant—very differently from the way their conquerors viewed them.

There is a gap of nearly 500 years between our day and that of the Aztec civilization at its height. Although much information on this rich and unusual way of life has been lost in that time, a substantial amount has been recovered.

Today we know about the Aztec civilization from three main sources of information: archaeology, historical documents, and ethnography. Archaeology uncovers and interprets objects left by earlier peoples in order to understand their ways of life, or cultures. Peoples of the past, like those of the present, leave pieces of their lives behind. These artifacts, known to scholars as *material culture*, may be found by archaeologists hundreds or even thousands of years later. Many things keep archaeologists from gaining full knowledge of ancient cultures. Some types of objects do not survive over the centuries, nor do those that last always remain in their original place. For instance, wood, cloth, feathers, and paper disintegrate; stones are taken from

The unearthing of the Great Temple or Templo Mayor *of Tenochtitlan.* *Excavations took place in downtown Mexico City in the late 1970s and early 1980s.*

buildings and reused to construct new buildings. Conquerors purposely destroy some features of the lives of those whom they have conquered. It is not always possible to excavate thoroughly in a particular location. Sites prized by archaeologists may be in the center of a major modern city or lie beneath a church or other structure. Ancient buildings may be damaged and artifacts stolen over the centuries. And important aspects of life, such as family relationships and government, are seldom represented directly by objects.

The material culture that the Aztecs left behind includes many large stone temples and monuments as well as stone, metal, and pottery artifacts. Of the perishable items, only fragments of clothing and a few feather ornaments still survive. The Spanish conquerors built their cities over the Aztec ones and dedicated their churches on the sites of Aztec temples. Today, stones from the Aztec capital city can sometimes be seen here and there in Spanish-period buildings in Mexico City.

Historical documents help fill in some of the gaps of information that archaeology cannot provide. Both the Spaniards and the native peoples of Mexico recorded information about the Aztec culture. The Aztecs wrote books in picture writing to record their histories, calendars, religious beliefs, censuses (population counts), taxes, and many other aspects of their lives. Unfortunately, only a few of these books remain and most are copies of the original versions, made after the Spanish

conquest. In the 16th century, after the Spaniards became the new rulers of the land, there was a great quantity of writing by Spaniards and Indians. Indians recorded lengthy histories from memory. They were also frequently in the courts, often to settle problems with one another over rights to land and ancient titles, and these disputes were written down in the Aztecs' language, Nahuatl (NA-watl). (Many records in picture writing were also recorded in the Spanish alphabet.) These and other writings provide clues to the Aztec way of life and tell us how the Aztecs viewed the world and themselves. However, we must be cautious about some claims because some Indian historians and claimants wrote in order to retain or gain titles and wealth.

Spanish conquerors and friars wrote at great length about the Aztecs. Of the conquerors, Bernal Díaz del Castillo provides one of the most important chronicles. In order to learn about the Aztec culture in the 16th century, some friars spent years with Aztec elders. Many of them learned the native language and recorded information on virtually all aspects of Aztec life. The most famous and thorough of these friars was Bernardino de Sahagún, who arrived in Mexico in 1529 and remained until his death in 1590. He wrote several works that described the Aztec culture to the Spaniards and introduced Christian beliefs to the Indians. Thorough though the friars were, they too had biases. They did not record everything, and they often wrote with the purpose

A Nahua Indian woman, a descendant of the Aztecs, weaves cloth on a backstrap loom, the same type of loom used by Aztec women. One end of the loom is tied to a stationary object and the other is secured by a strap that goes around the back of the weaver.

pects of Aztec life were almost completely hidden from their view, such as life in the Aztec homes.

Thus, as helpful as the Indian and Spanish documents are, there are still many missing pieces. Luckily, more of these gaps can be filled in because some traditions of the Aztecs continue with their descendants. Although these people no longer build temples, practice human sacrifice, or wear feathered warrior costumes, there are still nearly 1 million people in Mexico who speak some form of the Aztec language and retain some of the ancient customs. For example, many Indian women today weave cloth much as their Aztec ancestors did and can describe their craft in the Nahuatl language. Because few pieces of cloth survive archaeologically and few 16th-century descriptions of weaving were written, the present-day accounts help us to understand an important occupation of the past. This type of information is collected through ethnography, or the systematic description of existing human cultures or ways of life.

The search for a full understanding of the Aztec civilization is ongoing, and each year our knowledge grows as more artifacts are uncovered, documents translated, and Indians interviewed. There is much that we do know. We know that the Aztecs had a different name for themselves; they called themselves Mexica (Me-SHEE-ka). The name *Aztec* comes from a place called Aztlan, a semimythical location from which the Mexica traveled before

of stamping out the native religion and converting the Indians to Christianity.

The Spanish conquerors and administrators also described the native way of life. The conquerors were military men and therefore observed and described fortresses and armies but not births and marriages. Some Aztec customs were so foreign to the Spaniards that they failed to understand them and did not even note them. And some as-

Ethnic groups of central Mexico who lived in the area surrounding the Valley of Mexico before the Spaniards arrived: The Otomí (top left), Quaquata (bottom left), and Totonaca (right) peoples. (From the Florentine Codex)

they arrived in the Valley of Mexico in the 13th century. The Mexica wandered from city to city through this already populated area until they finally founded the city of Tenochtitlan on an island in Lake Texcoco in 1325. For the next 105 years, until 1430, they worked to become the most important military and political power in central Mexico. They formed a strong alliance with their neighbors to the east and west: the Acolhuaca (A-kol-WA-ka) of Texcoco (Tesh-KO-ko) and the Tepaneca (Te-pan-E-ka) of Tlacopan (Tla-KO-pan). By the time Motecuhzoma met Cortés in 1519, the Mexica, Acolhuaca, and Tepaneca had forged an enormous empire in Mexico, the Triple Alliance, or Aztec, Empire.

Today the term *Aztec* is used to refer to all the peoples of central Mexico who spoke related languages and shared similar customs. But in the early 16th century, the Aztec peoples did not con-

sider themselves a single unified body. Their first loyalties were to their own group; they thought of themselves as, for instance, Mexica, Tepaneca, or Acolhuaca.

The Valley of Mexico, which is now covered by a sprawling Mexico City, was the center of activity for the Mexica and their neighbors. This is where they built their greatest temples and organized their largest marketplaces. Here they celebrated their grandest rituals, with colorful processions and solemn rites. This is where the nobles lived in expensive palaces and merchants returning from long trading expeditions gave lavish feasts. Here the wise men studied the stars and history. And from the great cities of this valley the imperial armies marched, sometimes returning in glory, sometimes in defeat.

The valley covers about 2,772 square miles (7,000 square kilometers) in the central portion of Mexico and sits at an

(continued on page 22)

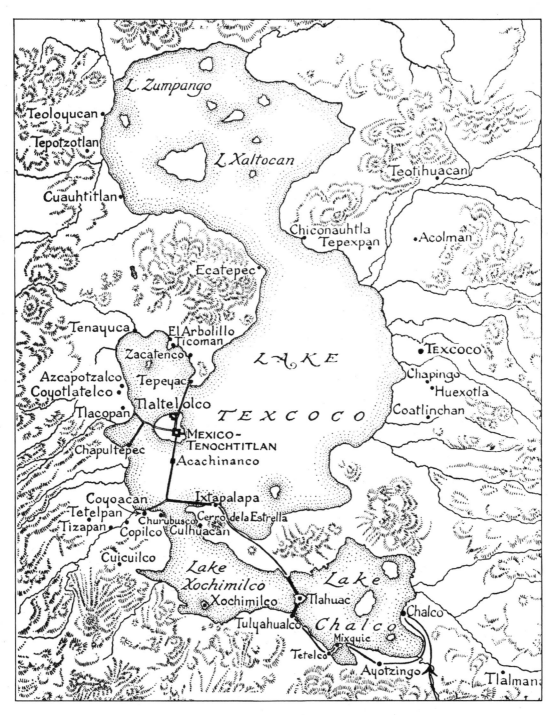

A reconstructed map of the Valley of Mexico showing the lakes, surrounding mountains, and cities that became part of the Aztec Empire.

PRONOUNCING
THE AZTEC LANGUAGE

The language spoken by the Aztecs was *Nahuatl* (NA-watl). Although no one today speaks the Classical Nahuatl of the Aztecs, many Mexicans do use modern dialects of Nahuatl (or Nahuat), which they usually call *Mexicano* (Me-shee-KA-no). These dialects give us clues to the pronunciation of the earlier language.

The word *Nahuatl* is related to another word that means clear and understandable sounds and speech. The Aztecs' language was first written in a phonetic alphabet in the 16th century by friars who came to Mexico after the Spanish explorers and conquerors. Because these friars spoke Spanish the pronunciation of the Classical Nahuatl that they recorded follows the rules of Spanish pronunciation, with a few exceptions.

The pronunciation of Aztec words follows these simple rules:

1. Stress or emphasis is almost always on the next-to-last syllable of a word.

2. Vowels are pronounced approximately as indicated below.

> **a** *as in English* **p**a**lm**   amatl (A-matl), paper
> **e** *as in English* **b**e**t**   tepetl (TE-petl), hill
> **i** *as in English* **s**ee   chilli (CHEE-lee), chile
> **o** *as in English* **s**o   tochtli (TOCH-tlee), rabbit

The vowel *u* usually follows *h* or *q* and is used in combination with another vowel. These combinations are pronounced as indicated below.

> **hua** *as in English* **wa**nder   huacalli (wa-KA-lee), a large basket
> **hue** *as in English* **wa**y   huexolotl (way-SHO-lotl), turkey
> **hui** *as in English* **wee**k   huictli (WEEK-tlee), digging stick
> **qua** *as in English* **qua**lity   qualli (KWA-lee), good
> **que** *as in English* **ke**pt   quechtli (KECH-tli), neck
> **qui** *as in English* **key**   oquichtli (o-KEECH-tlee), man

3. Most consonants are pronounced as in English or Spanish. Other consonants and their pronunciations are indicated below.

x *as in English* **she**	xochitl (SHO-cheetl), flower
z *as in English* **silly**	ozomatli (o-so-MA-tlee), monkey
ll *similar to English* **fill** but held longer	calli (KA-lee), house
tz *as in English* **cats**	tzontli (TSON-tlee), hair
tl *is a single sound, a* **t** *followed by a soft* **l**	coyotl (KO-yotl), coyote

The Spaniards had difficulty pronouncing *tl* at the end of words. It frequently became *te* (as in English *Te*d) when they spoke it, so that *tecolotl* (te-KO-lotl), the word for owl, became *tecolote* (te-ko-LO-te) and *ocotl* (O-kotl), the word for pine wood, became *ocote* (o-KO-te). *Xitomatl* (shee-TO-matl), which meant tomato, became *tomate* (to-MA-te).

Also, a *c* before an *a*, *o*, or a consonant is pronounced as a *k*; a *c* before *e* or *i* is pronounced as an *s*.

4. Nahuatl has a glottal stop. (This is a pause in speech sounding something like the expression "uh uh" in English and made by catching one's breath at the back of the throat.) The Spaniards who recorded Nahuatl often did not hear the sound, and only occasionally indicated it when they wrote it; when they indicated it, they usually used an *h*. However, *ohtli* (road), for instance, is most often written *otli*.

In 16th-century Europe, spelling rules were not as strict as they are today. For this reason, there was some variation in how the Spanish friars spelled the Aztec words they transcribed. For instance, the soldier Bernal Díaz del Castillo referred to Huitzilopochtli (Wee-tsee-lo-POCH-tlee) as Huichilobos (probably pronounced Wee-chee-LO-bos) and the name of the ruler Motecuhzoma (Mo-tek'w-SO-ma) may be seen as Montecuzoma, Mohtecuzoma, or, most often, Montezuma.

Ixtacihuatl (Sleeping Woman) Volcano, one of several volcanic mountains in central Mexico.

(continued from page 18)

elevation of over 7,000 feet (2,100 meters). It is almost completely surrounded by high mountains. The tallest snow-capped peaks reach elevations of over 17,000 feet (5,152 meters). Aside from the lofty peaks, the most notable natural feature of the valley when the Mexica occupied it was its lake system. (The lakes in this system are now almost completely drained.) Five interlocking lakes were filled from mountain runoff (streams formed from melting snow and rain water) and natural springs. However, because the water had no outlet to the sea, the people living on or near the lakes were often faced with floods.

Despite the hazards, the lakes and their shorelines and the surrounding hills and mountains offered an attractive setting and a comfortable way of living for large numbers of people. The lakes provided an efficient means of transportation. At the time of the Spanish conquest, the newly arrived Europeans marveled at the canoe congestion on the lakes. The lakes also provided a variety of food resources, such as fish, ducks, frogs, and large salamanders.

People living on the lakeshores collected grasses, which they dried and used to thatch the roofs of their houses or to weave into baskets or mats. They also worked at processing salt from the lakes. Using layers of mud and vegetation, they created land for cultivation in the shallow parts of the lakes, resulting in one of the most highly productive forms of agriculture ever developed.

At higher levels, inland from the lakes, villagers cultivated the staple crops of maize (corn), beans, squashes, and chiles (peppers). Town and city dwellers used stone to make tools, weapons, and sculptures and used local clay to make pottery. In the higher reaches of the mountains, people collected wood for firewood, building materials, weapons, and tools. All of these and many other activities took place in a relatively small area of central Mexico. Trade was important to distribute all of these goods throughout the region.

Beyond the Valley of Mexico lies a land of contrasts. Long mountain chains run parallel to the shores of the Pacific Ocean and the Gulf of Mexico. Hot tropical plains extend from the mountains to both shores. In northern Mexico, inland from the mountain ranges, stretch vast desert regions. South of the desert plateau, the center of Mexico begins to narrow. The mountains buckle and fold and there is a region of active volcanoes. Mountains surround the Valley of Mexico; to the east, south, and west lie endless mountains and more valleys.

The entire empire conquered by the Aztecs was situated within the zone between the Tropic of Cancer and the equator. But not all of the land was tropical in climate and vegetation. Enormous differences in elevation resulted in a great variety of plant and animal life, from mountain peak to valley to coastal plain. For example, at an elevation of 7,000 feet, the Valley of Mexico was in a region now referred to as *tierra fria*, or "cold land." In these highland regions, hardy crops can be grown, but the growing season is relatively short, and an early frost is always a threat.

Below the tierra fria regions is *tierra templada* (temperate land), at approximately 2,500 to 6,000 feet (750 to 1,800 meters) in elevation. This is a land of mountains and valleys that is ideal for agriculture. Below 2,500 feet, going down to sea level, stretches *tierra caliente* (hot land), including the coastal plains and low valleys. Tropical crops such as cotton, vanilla, and chocolate thrive in these hot and humid areas. These three zones lie close to one another, making it relatively easy for the wood collector of the cold lands to trade with the cotton grower of the hot lands.

This was the setting for the Mexica, who migrated from the northern deserts, settled in the Valley of Mexico, and sent armies to conquer large areas throughout Mexico. And this is the story of the Aztec civilization at its height in the early 16th century. It is a story about an amazing and exotic way of life; about a people who built enormous cities, fought many wars, designed delicate feather ornaments, and created beautiful poetry, all without the use of metal tools, the wheel, beasts of burden, or alphabetic writing. ▲

The Mexica were told to look for an eagle perching on a cactus as a sign that they had reached the place where they were to settle. The seated figures surrounding it represent early Mexica leaders. The border is made up of symbols that represent 51 consecutive years in the Aztec calendar. (From the Codex Mendoza)

FROM
TRIBE
TO
EMPIRE

The Mexica were just one of many civilizations in Mexico's prehistory. These civilizations existed as far back as approximately 1500 B.C. Among these were the Mayas and Toltecs.

The earliest of these civilizations, the Olmec, was centered along the Gulf Coast of Mexico and is considered the mother culture for later Mexican civilizations. The Olmecs worshiped many gods and built temples for them. They also built ceremonial centers, which contained important public and religious buildings but few houses, and developed a calendar for recording time and planning events. Their workers specialized in particular tasks, such as working fine stones, studying the stars, organizing religious ceremonies, or farming. The Olmecs' agricultural system was so productive that some individuals did not have to farm at all but could eat the excess of what the farmers produced. To obtain food, they traded their specialized goods or services, such as pottery, medical treatment, or a religious service. The result was a social system in which some people were more wealthy and powerful than others. The Olmecs traded not just within the general area of a ceremonial center but over long distances. They were well connected with other people living in many parts of Mexico.

Long before the Spaniards had encountered the Aztecs, many civilizations rose and fell. Between about A.D. 300 and 900 the so-called Classic Maya civilization developed in southern Mexico and Guatemala. The Maya built lofty temples and further developed calendars and hieroglyphics (picture script). In central Mexico, close to present-day Mexico City, Teotihuacan (Te-o-tee-WA-kan) grew to be a large city, complete with suburbs. It spread over 20 square miles and is estimated to have housed more than 125,000 people. Like the Olmecs and Classic Mayas, the so-called Teotihuacanos produced product surpluses, had specialized jobs, traded goods widely, had differences in wealth

25

A stairway at the base of the Temple of Quetzalcoatl in Teotihuacan. The serpent heads are symbols of the god Quetzalcoatl. The city of Teotihuacan dominated the Valley of Mexico long before the Mexica rose to power. It was the first truly urban site in central Mexico.

and power, and worshiped many gods. They also used calendars and built large public buildings.

However, by A.D. 750, Teotihuacan was no longer as important or glorious a city as it had once been. It would be replaced in central Mexico by several new cities. These cities maintained the earlier ways of living, but tended to be more militaristic (aggressively oriented toward war). Some of the people set their cities on hilltops, producing for-tresslike communities, and they often warred among themselves. The most important of these cities was Tollan (or Tula), home of the powerful Toltecs. When Tollan fell in the late 1100s, some of its survivors moved into the Valley of Mexico. Descendants of these leaders continued to be respected by other groups in central Mexico for centuries.

From the fall of Tollan until the cre-ation of the Aztec Empire, many cities and towns competed with one another for control of the Valley of Mexico. When the Mexica arrived in the 13th century, the valley around the lakes was well populated. In addition to the Toltec survivors and other ancient set-tlers, many groups similar to the Mexica had migrated south into the valley and settled there.

While early Mexican civilizations were prospering in central and south-ern Mexico, many tribal groups were living in the northern deserts. The Mex-ica were among them. These people were collectively called Chichimeca (Chee-chee-ME-ka), or "People of the Dog." These tribal groups practiced lit-tle or no agriculture in their dry envi-ronment. They lived by hunting small animals and collecting wild plants. The people lived together in relatively small groups and moved frequently in search of food resources.

Over a period of several hundred years, many of the Chichimec tribes moved farther and farther south, away from the dry deserts. According to the ancient myths and histories, the Mexica migration extended from about A.D. 1111 to 1325. The tribe's migrations be-gan from Aztlan, the "Place of the Her-ons," which was probably somewhere

The Toltec Temple of Quetzalcoatl at Tollan (Tula). The four warrior statues originally served as roof supports for the temple sanctuary on top of the platform. Tollan was a major urban center in central Mexico until it was abandoned as the capital of the Toltec Empire and subsequently destroyed in the late 1100s.

northwest of the Valley of Mexico. From Aztlan they traveled to Chicomoztoc (Chee-ko-MOS-tok), or "Seven Caves." Several other Chichimec tribes gathered here, and many then left and settled in the Valley of Mexico before the Mexica.

The Mexica were the last to leave the region of the caves, according to their histories. During their long journey, they adopted some of the central Mexican customs that they encountered. In addition to hunting and gathering for food, they learned to cultivate corn, chiles, and other crops. They followed the calendars developed by the central Mexican civilizations. They also had

priests who, according to the histories, guided the tribal Mexica on their journey. Wherever they stopped, the people built a temple for their most important god, their patron Huitzilopochtli (Wee-tsee-lo-POCH-tlee). This god, through the priests, had told them to search for a sign that would show them where to settle. It was a long and difficult trip, partly because the people had many disagreements among themselves. In one incident, a faction decided to remain at a pleasant spot rather than proceed on their journey as their god commanded; their decision led to severe internal violence.

Toltec limestone relief sculpture showing an eagle devouring a human heart. The eagle represents the sun. There were many relief panels showing eagles at the Temple of Quetzalcoatl in Tollan. The Mexica admired Toltec artisans and adopted many symbols from Toltec culture.

When they arrived in the Valley of Mexico, there was little available land on which to settle. The people already living in the valley had their own alliances and other political, religious, and social arrangements. The Mexica's entrance into this well-established situation was both unspectacular and unwelcomed. They were not popular, and some of their unusual customs and abilities, such as being able to thrive in a rocky place inhabited by snakes, terrified the city dwellers. Seeking a permanent home, they moved from city to city, guided by Huitzilopochtli.

Finally, after a particularly bad day, they were chased out into one of the five lakes in the valley, Lake Texcoco, where they took refuge on an island. There, according to Mexica histories, they saw an eagle standing on a cactus, grasping a snake in its mouth. This was the sign they had been looking for, and they ended their long journey. The year was 1325. The Mexica named the site Tenochtitlan, "Place of the Prickly Pear Cactus Fruit." In the 15th and 16th centuries, it would grow into one of the world's largest cities.

On their small island, the Mexica faced numerous problems. One of these was how to survive with so many powerful groups surrounding them. The land they had settled on was bounded by three city-states (small political units whose major activities took place in one large city with many villages and towns surrounding it): Texcoco, Culhuacan, and Azcapotzalco (As-ka-pot-SAL-ko). In addition, there were no natural sources of substantial building materials, such as stone or wood, which the people needed to build homes and a temple for their god. One solution solved both problems: The Mexica were known to be fierce and clever warriors, and they offered their military services to Azcapotzalco, one of the most powerful of the lakeside cities. In their capacity as soldiers, the Mexica could hold a legitimate position among the rulers and city-dwellers of the area. This also opened up trading opportunities. They could exchange their lake products, such as fish and small aquatic animals, for building materials and other necessary goods.

As they became accepted by other groups in the valley, the Mexica tried to develop additional political alliances. They did this most effectively by arranging marriages of their leaders to the daughters of nearby rulers. One such marriage—between the Mexica ruler Acamapichtli (A-ka-ma-PEECH-tlee) and a Culhua (KOL-wa) princess from the neighboring city of Culhuacan— tied the Mexica to the prestigious Toltecs.

The first project of the Mexica on their newfound island was to build a temple to their god Huitzilopochtli. The temple was, at first, a small and simple altar, but it would grow throughout the next two centuries as the Mexica became more populous and prosperous. Every Mexica ruler added to it. A temple for the rain god Tlaloc (TLA-lok) was attached in the 14th century to the temple to Huitzilopochtli. The platform and base on which these temples rested were enlarged many times. Eventually the structure reached 200 feet (60 meters) in height. When the Spaniards first saw the temple they were amazed by its size and grandeur.

Three large causeways were built across the lake to connect the island city to the cities on the mainland. One causeway stretched to the south, another north, and another west. Although a large part of the traffic from city to city was by canoe across the lake,

these causeways provided foot access to and from Tenochtitlan. Aqueducts also extended to the city, carrying fresh spring water to the thousands of urban inhabitants.

As their population grew, the Mexica soon ran out of living space on their island. They solved this problem by creating *chinampas*, or so-called floating gardens, around the island. The Mexica learned how to build chinampas from their neighbors on the lakes. The chinampas have been misnamed because these extremely fertile plots did not actually float. They were pieces of land created by piling up alternating layers of vegetation and mud in the shallow marshy parts of the lakes. Chinampas

Chinampas *near Mexico City today. The Aztecs built up these fertile plots of land in the shallow lake areas with alternating layers of vegetation and mud.*

were held in place, at first by posts and later by the roots of willow trees, at the corners and along the sides of the plots. When the layers of vegetation and mud were piled up higher than the water level, they were ready for cultivation. The chinampas were laid out in a grid pattern; each plot was a rectangle about 30 feet by 330 feet (9.14 by 100.58 meters) bordered by canals and walkways. The crops were easily watered by simply scooping out water from the canal. The creation of the chinampas resulted in a city of canals full of canoe traffic.

Chinampas added both living and agricultural space to the island. Houses could be built on chinampas after they were firmly in place, and the plots were used to grow a great variety of products, from maize and beans to tomatoes and flowers. The Mexica built chinampas all around Tenochtitlan, like their neighbors in the freshwater lakes to the south. They were, however, constantly faced with the danger of flooding, which brought salty water across the chinampas and ruined the land and crops. Lake Texcoco accumulated minerals from the river water running into it, which caused the water to be brackish. In the mid-15th century, this problem was solved; a dike was built, separating the western section of the lake where Tenochtitlan was located and protecting the city from salty water and some flooding.

As the city grew, the number of temples, palaces, schools, ball courts, and other public buildings in it grew as well.

A map of the island city of Tenochtitlan from Cortés's second letter to the Spanish emperor Charles V. The map was published in 1524. The map shows the central plaza, the causeways that linked the city to the mainland cities, and the dike (right) that was built to protect the city from floods.

It is estimated that by the time the Spaniards arrived in 1519, the city's population was 150,000 to 200,000. It would have been one of the largest cities in the world at that time. The first Spaniards to view it were amazed. One conqueror, Bernal Díaz del Castillo, wrote:

When we saw so many cities and villages built on the water and other great towns on dry land and that straight and level Causeway going towards Mexico [Tenochtitlan], we were amazed and said that it was like the enchantments they tell of in the legend of Amadis, on account of the great towers and cues [temples] and buildings rising from the water, and all built of masonry. And some of our soldiers even asked whether the things that we saw were not a dream.

At the center of the city was the main ceremonial district, a huge plaza surrounded by a *coatepantli*, or wall of carved serpents. Within this enclosure, the most dominant structure was the great temple of Huitzilopochtli and Tlaloc. In addition, there were temples to other gods, schools run by priests, and a ball court. Nearby were multi-roomed palaces of rulers and nobles. Just north of this great plaza was the community of Tlatelolco (Tla-te-LOL-ko), another Mexica settlement and the location of the largest marketplace of the realm. Here virtually all products of the land were sold, including food, cloth, tools, and precious stones.

The rest of the city was divided into residential districts, which could be compared to suburbs. Every district had

The main ceremonial district of Tenochtitlan in a drawing of a mid-20th-century reconstruction. The Great Temple of Huitzilopochtli and Tlaloc dominates the plaza, which is surrounded by a wall decorated with carved serpents. Ceremonies were held on the platforms below the temple, and a variety of public events, including games, took place in the plaza.

its own plaza, complete with temple, school, and other religious and political offices. By the time of the Spanish conquest, Tenochtitlan sprawled over about 4.75 square miles (12 square kilometers) and may have contained as many as 80 districts. The residents of each district all belonged to the same *calpulli* (kal-PO-lee), an organization that served social, religious, economic, and political functions. Each calpulli had communally held land and its own patron god whom its members honored in special ceremonies. Each calpulli also had a leader, the *calpulec*, who organized work on public projects, such as building temples, and made sure that taxes to the ruler were paid. The men from a calpulli fought together in battle.

While building their city, the Mexica learned many skills and techniques from their neighbors in the valley, who in their turn had carried on the patterns established in earlier civilizations. The Mexica produced large surpluses from their fertile lands and had many specialists; some produced crafts, whereas others served as merchants, priests, or government officials. Huge caravans of merchants traveled great distances, trading to obtain the most valued commodities: gold, fine stones, and precious tropical feathers. They worshiped many gods and frequently held colorful religious ceremonies. And they built an empire.

In their first hundred years at Tenochtitlan, the Mexica remained subservient to the rulers of the neighboring city of Azcapotzalco. Their primary service was military assistance, but they also paid taxes. They were excellent warriors and sometimes were given land as a reward for their efforts. By the 15th century, the Mexica had become powerful in their own right. They not only possessed a mighty fighting force but had also established strong political and economic ties with other cities in the valley.

In 1426 the Mexica got into a dispute with Azcapotzalco and several other neighboring cities. These neighbors may have been offended by the way in which the Mexica requested help in building an aqueduct to provide more water to Tenochtitlan. As a result, the people of Azcapotzalco and the surrounding region blockaded the city and sent assassins to kill the Mexica ruler, Chimalpopoca, and his son. Tensions grew into a war that lasted from 1428 to 1430. The Mexica, along with the Acolhuaca of Texcoco, ultimately defeated the Tepanecas of Azcapotzalco. This victory made the two cities the new rulers of the valley. They joined with a third, Tlacopan, located to the west of Tenochtitlan, and formed a military alliance. This Triple Alliance set out to conquer its neighbors in the valley and far beyond, forging the Aztec Empire.

For the next 90 years, the Triple Alliance was almost constantly at war. Its armies usually returned victorious, but they also suffered some major defeats. They were never able to conquer their powerful neighbors to the west, the

MEXICO, 1519

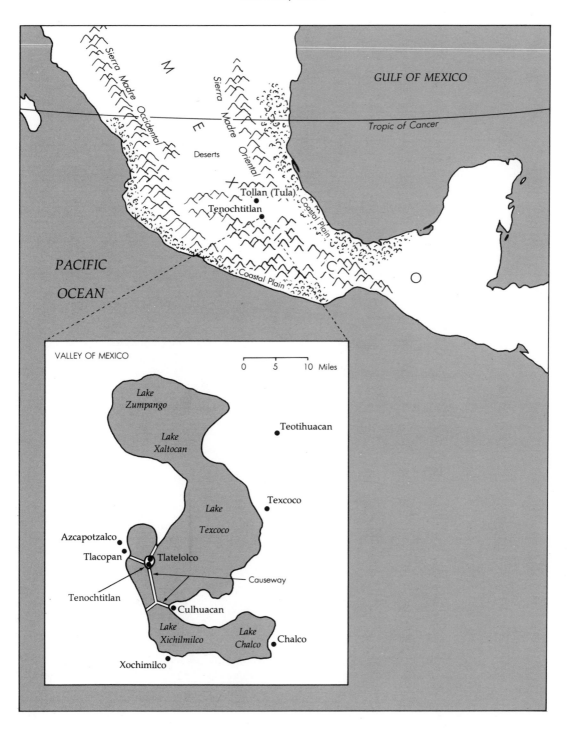

GULF OF MEXICO

Sierra Madre Occidental

Sierra Madre Oriental

M E

Deserts

Tropic of Cancer

Tollan (Tula)

Tenochtitlan

Coastal Plain

PACIFIC

OCEAN

Coastal Plain

VALLEY OF MEXICO

0   5   10 Miles

Lake
Zumpango

Teotihuacan

Lake
Xaltocan

Lake

Texcoco

Texcoco

Azcapotzalco

Tlacopan

Tlatelolco

Causeway

Tenochtitlan

Culhuacan

Lake
Xichilmilco

Lake
Chalco

Chalco

Xochimilco

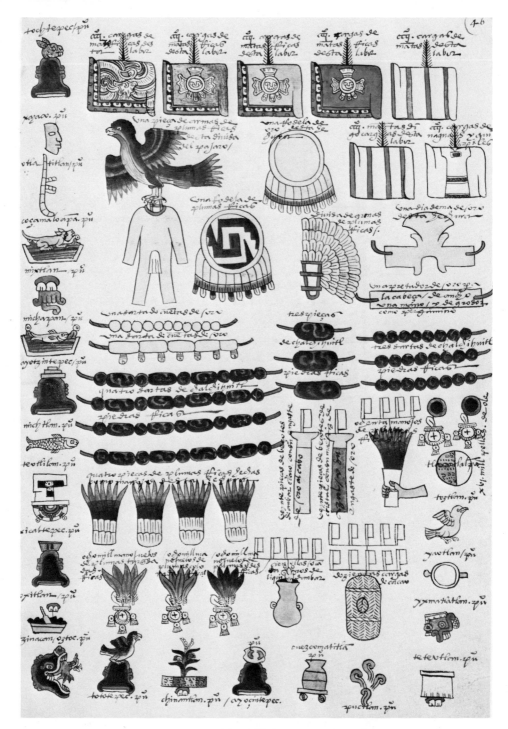

Items sent as tribute to the Aztecs from the Gulf Coast province of Tochtepec. This rich province gave fine decorated clothing (top), *warriors' costumes, gold ornaments* (center left), *strings of jade beads* (center), *thousands of feathers* (lower left), *and chocolate* (lower right, within basket). *(From the* Codex Mendoza)

Tarascans. And although they fought many wars against the city-state of Tlaxcalla (Tlash-KA-lah), the Aztec army could not overwhelm that of the Tlaxcallans.

The defeated peoples were required to pay tribute in the form of specific goods. Most often the Aztecs demanded clothing, followed by requests for foods such as maize, beans, and chiles. From the hot lands they received cotton, cacao, precious feathers, and jaguar skins. From other areas the Aztecs demanded gold, copper, turquoise, honey, firewood, and many other items.

By demanding tribute the Aztecs were able to exercise control over the supply of certain desired luxuries that were not found naturally in the Valley of Mexico. Tropical feathers, gold, fine stones, and other rare materials were in demand because they were signs of wealth and social position. Only the wealthiest and most prestigious people, the nobles, could wear gold lip plugs (a piece of jewelry worn on the lower lip), feather headdresses, or richly decorated cotton capes. By law, commoners could not wear such items, even if they somehow became able to afford them.

The conquered peoples had to pay tribute regularly, usually four times each year. The Aztecs sent officials to each conquered province for the purpose of collecting these treasures. Aside from sending out the often-feared tribute collectors, the Aztecs usually left the provinces alone. The native ruler of an area could continue to rule, as long as tribute flowed into Tenochtitlan and the area did not rebel. But rebellions were quite frequent. When a province rebelled and was reconquered, its tribute payments were doubled, according to Diego Durán, a Dominican friar who arrived in Mexico in about 1542 and wrote extensively on the Aztecs and their culture.

Over a span of 200 years, the Mexica had grown from a tribe to an empire. Along the way they adopted many customs and patterns already present in Mexico, but they also gave these customs their own stamp. They practiced warfare and human sacrifice on a scale unequaled by any other group before them. They also produced works of art that were monumental and powerful and others that were delicate and sensitive; and they were skilled engineers, architects, lawmakers, and poets. ▲

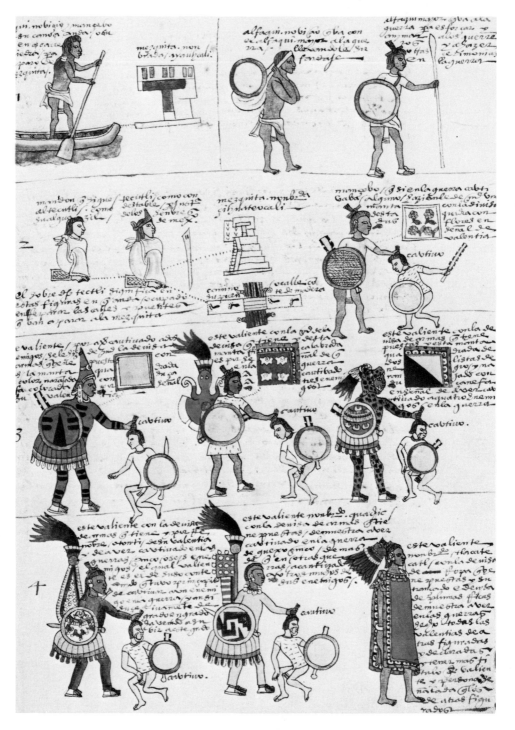

A page of the Codex Mendoza *shows how a warrior gained status in Aztec society by capturing enemy warriors. After each capture was made, the warrior gained a distinctly decorated cape and warrior costume, which indicated his new status.*

THE
MEXICA WAY
OF
LIFE

The Mexica viewed themselves as traveling in life along a mountain peak. On either side of the peak was a deep canyon. Straying from the straight path would result in a fall into the canyon. Only moderation and caution in all things would prevent one from tumbling.

To help them stay on the path, the Mexica were guided by rules of behavior in all that they did. These rules defined appropriate and inappropriate actions and set standards, goals, and ideals for living. In addition to rules about everyday behavior, the Mexica had rules relating to their position in society. People belonged to social classes based on the class of their parents and on their own personal achievements. The basic social division was between nobles and commoners. However, certain specialists, especially merchants and artisans of expensive luxury goods, occupied intermediate positions.

Although the rules of behavior varied somewhat according to the position one held in Mexica society, everyone was expected to follow the ideal of the "exemplary life." The attainment of this ideal required obedience, honesty, respect, moderation, modesty, and energy.

Friar Sahagún reported that a nobleman, for example, would instruct his son to follow eight specific rules:

1. Do not sleep too much, or you will become a sleeper, a dreamer.

2. Be careful in your travels. Go peacefully and quietly, and do not throw your feet or go jumping, or you will be called a fool and shameless.

3. Speak very slowly. Do not speak fast, do not pant or squeak, or you will be called a groaner, a growler, a squeaker.

4. Do not stare into another person's face.

5. Do not eavesdrop and do not gossip.

6. When you are called, do not be called twice or you will be thought lazy or rebellious. This is when you will be struck with the club and the stone.

7. Do not dress vainly, or decorate yourself fantastically; dress carefully so you do not trip over your cape. Also, do not shorten your cape or expose your shoulders.

8. Above all, drink and eat in moderation. Do not eat too much food; eat slowly, calmly and quietly.

Men, women, and children had general rules to live by in order to fulfill their duties in their respective roles. The Mexica man, as father and husband, was responsible for the well-being of his household. He was the provider and administrator of the household's property, the adviser and teacher of his children. It was particularly important that a man be thrifty, energetic, and caring and that he not squander the family's property through gambling, laziness, or carelessness. If he was a nobleman, much of his time and energy was spent on duties outside the household. He might be a government official, scribe (person who produced written records), or teacher. He was also expected to be a fierce and courageous warrior and a leader in battle. If he was a commoner, he must be an energetic farmer, fisherman, or craftsman. He was responsible for supporting his family through hard work and supporting the government through payment of his taxes. Like the nobleman, he must be eager to go to war and be fearless on the battlefield.

The Mexica woman, as mother and wife, devoted most of her time and energy to the everyday running of the household. Ideally, she was hardworking and attentive and spent much of her time educating her daughters. Whether noblewoman or commoner, a woman was expected to become skilled in weaving cloth and preparing food. The noblewoman, however, typically managed the household. Her servants did the cleaning, cooking, and marketing. The commoner, described by Sahagún as robust, vigorous, and energetic, would handle all these chores with the aid of her daughters and any other female relatives in the household.

The Mexica child was expected to be respectful, obedient, and humble. Chil-

Aztec women's duties included weaving cloth. They used a backstrap loom and fiber made from maguey, yucca, and cotton plants. (From the Florentine Codex)

Noblewomen in the decorated tunics and skirts that were their everyday clothing. (From the Florentine Codex)

dren were frequently lectured by their parents and other adults about correct behavior.

People in each of the social classes had to follow rules that set forth their specific privileges and duties. There were even rules that specified the clothing and adornment appropriate for members of each class. For example, only a ruler, the highest rank within the noble class, could wear the most expensive decorated cotton cloaks. Other nobles could wear less extravagant cloaks. Commoners could wear only

the simplest clothing, made of coarsely woven maguey (a spiny-leaved plant) or yucca (a plant with rigid, fibrous leaves) fibers.

Nobles and commoners also wore their clothes differently. The cloak of a male commoner could not reach below the knee, unless as a warrior he had been wounded on his legs. Friar Durán wrote:

> And so it was that when one encountered a person who wore his mantle [cloak] longer than the laws permitted, one immediately looked at his legs. If he had wounds acquired in war he would be left in peace, and if he did not, he would be killed. They would say, "Since that leg did not flee from the sword, it is just that it be rewarded and honored."

In addition, only the ruler and other nobles could wear ornaments such as gold headbands with feathers, gold armbands, or lip, ear, and nose plugs made of precious metals and stones. And only the nobles could build two-

Drummers and dancers performing at a special celebration. (From the Florentine Codex)

Gold lip plug in the form of a serpent (2 5/8 inches long, 2 1/2 inches high). Only people of the noble class could own and wear this type of jewelry.

story houses; commoners' houses could be only one story high. The existence of these signs meant that one's position in Mexica society was readily visible. But there were other differences as well.

The nobility controlled most of the wealth in the society. They owned their own land and in many ways controlled the lives of the people who worked on the land. Commoners had to pay taxes or tribute to local nobles or to the city-state, and supplied nobles' households with food, clothing, firewood, and other necessary goods.

Nobles and commoners had very different standards of living and celebrated life-cycle events such as births and weddings in different ways. For example, the naming ceremony of an in-

fant born into a noble family—and especially the feast thereafter—was elaborate. The banquet began with the giving of an abundance of tobacco and flowers to the guests. Then came the distribution of large amounts of food and *cacahuatl* (ka-KA-watl), a hot chocolate drink that was highly valued. Entertainment, especially singing and joking, closed the feasting.

This same event was celebrated by commoners, but in a much simpler fashion. Sahagún reported that

> among the poor folk, among the workers of the fields and the water folk . . . only miserably, in poverty and want, were receptions and invitations made. . . . Many things were omitted or spoiled . . . perhaps only old, withered flowers could he [the commoner] find or come by; perhaps only leftover, bitter sauces, and stale tamales and tortillas were offered them.

The social class system of the Mexica was complex and strictly maintained. The basic classes of nobles and commoners were subdivided even further. At the top of the noble class were the rulers, *tlatoque* (tla-TO-ke), who held the highest offices. The position of ruler was inherited, sometimes by the ruler's brother before passing to the ruler's son. There were usually several men who were eligible for the position. In Tenochtitlan a small, elite group, consisting of certain high-ranking chiefs,

NOBILITY		
Rulers	tlatoani (singular) tlatoque (plural)	Ruled empires, cities, or major towns
Chiefs	tecutli (singular) tetecutin (plural)	Controlled a more limited area than rulers; usually held high military positions
Nobles	pilli (singular) pipiltin (plural)	Held governmental, religious, and military positions
INTERMEDIATE POSITIONS		
Merchants	pochtecatl (singular) pochtecah (plural)	Traded luxury goods and foods over long distances; were organized into guilds; often served as spies
Luxury artisans	toltecatl (singular) toltecah (plural)	Made fine handcrafts such as sculpture, mosaic, gold-, and featherwork
COMMONERS		
Free commoners	macehualli (singular) macehualtin (plural)	Worked at agriculture, fishing, and producing everyday crafts; organized into calpulli
Rural tenants	mayeque (singular and plural)	Worked on the private lands of the nobility
Slaves	tlacotli (singular) tlacotin (plural)	Provided urban labor for the nobility; became slaves through gambling, poverty, or a criminal act

Aztec social classes were largely hereditary. Children of rulers and chiefs were nobles by birth, and only nobles could become rulers and chiefs. There was, however, some possibility of upward movement: Lower-ranked nobles who distinguished themselves in battle could rise to higher ranks; commoners who served with military distinction could become advisers to rulers; and slaves could buy their freedom. The slave class was not hereditary; indebtedness and criminal activity could reduce persons of higher rank to slavery.

warriors, officials, and priests, would select the new ruler, or *tlatoani*. The tlatoani would go through an elaborate ritual to be properly installed. Then he would usually organize a great war and lead his armies into battle. A successful campaign, complete with enemy captives for sacrifice, was a sign that the ruler's reign would be a glorious one.

Within the small and privileged group of tlatoque, there were several levels or ranks: the Triple Alliance emperors, rulers of large city-states, and rulers of smaller cities or towns. The

A 15 1/2-inch basalt sculpture of a macehualli, *or commoner. The figure may have served as a flag bearer.*

three corulers of the Triple Alliance were the highest and most powerful government officials and they enjoyed extraordinary styles of living. They dressed in rich and elegant clothes, had large palaces and numerous slaves, and enjoyed hunting game and birds for sport and being entertained by jugglers, acrobats, and jesters. They also ate well. Sahagún claimed that each day the Mexica emperor Motecuhzoma was served

> two thousand kinds of various foods; hot tortillas, white tamales with beans forming a sea shell on top; red tamales; the main meal of roll-shaped tortillas and many (foods): sauces with turkeys, quails, venison, rabbit, hare, rat, lobster, small fish, large fish; then all (manner of) sweet fruits.

This style of life was not as carefree as it may appear. The ruler had many responsibilities. He had to guard his territory, whether city-state or town; organize wars and other military activities (calling men to war on his behalf); sponsor religious celebrations to benefit his political unit; and decide some legal cases. He was also supposed to be a great speaker. The title *tlatoani* means speaker. In addition, he was always expected to be generous. A successful ruler was supposed to be a

> protector; one who carries (his subjects) in his arms, who unites them. . . . He rules, takes responsibilities, assumes burdens. He carries (his subjects) in his cape . . . he is obeyed. (To him) as shelter, as refuge, there is recourse.

There were many other categories of nobles in the society. One contained chiefs, or *tetecutin* (te-TEK'W-teen). They owned large estates, were frequently advisers to a ruler, or served as judges, generals, or tax collectors. Because only one son (or brother) of a ruler could succeed him, the others, still high-ranking nobles, were given these prestigious positions. Like rulers, they owned their own lands and received goods and services from the commoners who worked those lands.

A category of lower-ranking nobles comprised the other sons of rulers and chiefs. They had the same rights as all nobles but were usually not as powerful or wealthy as rulers or chiefs. Rarely did they own large estates but instead served as lower-level government or military officials, teachers, priests, astrologers, or scribes.

Most people in Aztec society were commoners, or *macehualtin* (ma-se-WAL-teen). They were the farmers, fishermen, and crafters of useful goods such as pottery and mats. In addition, commoners constituted the main body of the Aztec armies. They were trained in the military arts and were always ready to go to war. Most commoners were members of calpulli (groupings of people who lived together in a specific district). Records indicate that the lands that calpulli members farmed were run by the calpulli themselves. Each married male of a calpulli was allotted land to farm. Members occasionally had to work as laborers for the city on public projects such as building a road or a temple.

A carved stone figure of a man holding a squash. Squash was just one crop cultivated by the commoners. Some commoners worked on communally owned land; others worked on land owned by nobles.

A detail from the Florentine Codex *shows child and adult slaves.*

Another group of commoners were the *mayeque* (ma-YE-ke). These were the landless peasants who were not members of calpulli but who worked instead on nobles' privately owned lands. Their responsibilities and way of life were very much like those of other commoners, but their duties were always directed to the noble they served, whether in farming fields, weaving cloth, or providing firewood.

Ill fortune could bring anyone to the position of slave, or *tlacotli* (tla-KO-tlee). A person could become a tlacotli by committing a theft; by failing to pay tribute or gambling debts; or by extreme poverty. Slaves owed their labor to another person but were not themselves owned by those whom they served. They kept most of their personal free-

doms, could marry as others did, and could hold property. Some slaves even had other slaves. With few exceptions, a slave's children were born free.

People could also sell themselves or their children into slavery. This was done as a way of surviving misfortune and was most likely to happen at a time of famine. From 1450 to 1454, the Valley of Mexico suffered a disastrous famine, and many Mexica, in despair, sold themselves or their children into slavery to people living near the Gulf Coast of Mexico. In exchange for their services, they or their families received maize, which still grew plentifully in these hot, humid lands.

Slaves were bought and sold in the marketplaces, and some of the wealthiest merchants were those who traded in slaves. Professional merchants, *pochtecah* (poch-TE-kah), along with artisans of fine luxuries, *toltecah* (tol-TE-kah) occupied an intermediate position in Aztec society. A *pochtecatl* or a *toltecatl* was not born into nobility but could, and often did, become as wealthy as a noble. Merchants went on long trips by caravan to distant lands to trade for such items as tropical feathers, gold, fine stones, and jaguar skins. Nobles paid handsomely for these luxuries. Although the merchants could become very wealthy, they still had to dress humbly because they were not nobles. Among themselves, however, they would hold magnificent feasts.

A great feast was held to mark a merchant's success and to gain status

A merchant and a woman, probably his wife, prepare for a feast. Enormous quantities of food, such as turkey, were served and gifts of baskets, bowls, and cloth distributed at these feasts. (From the Florentine Codex)

among fellow merchants. After several profitable trading missions, a merchant might feel wealthy enough to put on a feast, at which he would offer only the finest food, flowers, and tobacco. If the merchant were able to provide lavishly, the event was considered a success, and he would be raised to a higher position within the merchant guild.

The toltecah fashioned the luxury materials brought back by merchants into fancy fans, headdresses, jewelry, and other objects. Luxury artisans and merchants seem to have been organized much like the guilds of medieval Europe (11th to 15th century). Members of these Aztec guilds lived in separate calpulli, worshiped their own patron gods, celebrated special religious ceremonies, and provided for the education and training of their children. As individuals learned a craft, they moved up from apprentice to master. At each level, the individual produced more and more complicated pieces and became wealthier and wealthier. Sometimes the toltecah were employed by rulers and sometimes they worked independently, selling their creations in the marketplaces.

The Aztec social class system somewhat resembles a caste system, in which a person's place in life is determined at birth and movement up or down the social ladder is almost impossible. In Aztec society, however,

Women prepared the food for the members of their household. Corn was a staple in the Aztec diet. In this detail from the Florentine Codex a woman is making cornmeal with a mano *on a* metate, *utensils that are still used today in Mexico.*

there were a few possibilities for social and economic mobility. For example, a commoner could occasionally dedicate a child to a school for the nobles. In this case, parents made a vow when a child was young that they would later bring the child to the noble school. This would provide the child with an education that could lead to an occupation at the lower levels of the noble class, such as astrologer, scribe, or teacher.

But the best and most used way to climb the social ladder was by showing courage in battle. A primary object of warfare was to capture enemy warriors for sacrifice. The more captives a Mexica took, the more privileges he was granted. After taking four captives, a warrior, whether noble or commoner, was entitled to sit on the ruler's war council, an important military body that advised the ruler when and where to wage a war and on other military matters. A warrior who was especially brave could join a knightly order—the Eagles, Jaguars, Otomís, or Cuachic—whose members often led the armies into battle. Although some commoners could become famous as warriors and earn many privileges, they could not become true nobles.

With all the rules of behavior and a strict social class system to guide them, the Mexica went about their daily activities. On a typical day, they would rise at dawn and immediately begin to work. They would typically have a mid-morning meal of *atolli* (maize gruel) for commoners or cacahuatl for nobles. Then they would return to work, eating their main meal with their family at midday. The Mexica enjoyed a variety of foods. They were extremely fond of maize *tamales*, ground corn dough filled with various ingredients and baked inside corn husks. They prepared them with imagination. According to Sahagún there were

> white tamales with beans forming a
> sea shell on top . . . tamales of maize
> softened in wood ashes . . . tamales
> of meat cooked with maize and
> yellow chili . . . tamales made of

maize flowers with ground amaranth seed and cherries added . . . tamales made with honey.

Maize was central in the Aztec diet, but the Aztecs also ate beans, many kinds of chiles (from mild to very hot), squashes, tomatoes, cactus fruits, and other fruits and vegetables. These foods were supplemented with wild and domesticated animals. Deer, rabbits, and other animals were hunted. The lakes and rivers were full of fish and many kinds of edible birds, especially ducks. The turkey and dog were domesticated and eaten. Sahagún described one large and expensive merchant feast where the host

> provided turkeys, perhaps eighty or a hundred of them. Then he bought dogs to provide the people as food, perhaps twenty or forty . . . they put them with the turkeys which they served; at the bottom of the sauce dish they placed the dog meat, on top they placed the turkey as required.

A great many other foods were gathered from the environment. These included locusts, grubs, fish eggs, lizards, honey, and *tecuitlatl* (te-KWEE-tlatl), a green lake scum formed by water-fly eggs. The Spanish soldier Díaz del Castillo wrote that the people made a cake from it that was cheeselike in flavor.

As is still true today in Mexico, people would relax for a few hours in the early afternoon, when the heat of the day was greatest. Then they would return to work for the remainder of the afternoon. The Mexica probably enjoyed a light evening meal, retiring on their sleeping mats shortly after sunset.

This daily routine varied somewhat according to a person's social class, occupation, gender, and age. The activities of the farmers and fishermen changed with the seasons. Priests could be up at all hours of the night, offering incense and sacrifices to the gods. And warriors kept watch over the city on day and night shifts, checking for any military threat. ▲

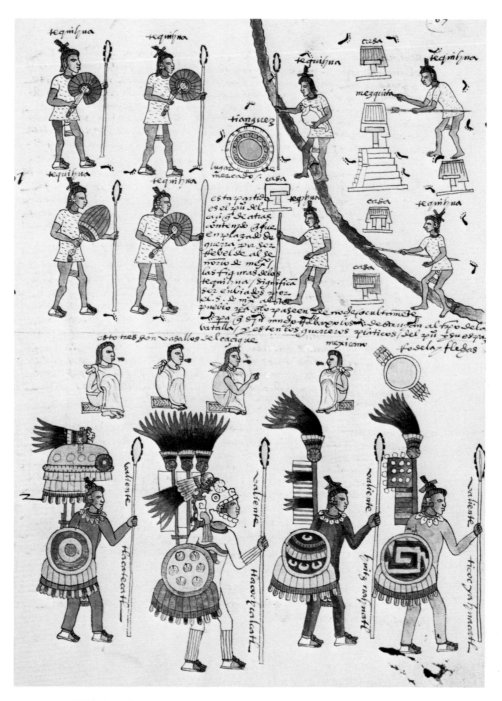

*Warriors dressed in quilted cotton armor prepare for battle (top),
while negotiations to prevent war are conducted (center). Warriors
who had captured many enemies and been courageous in battle could
become high-ranking career officers (center) and were rewarded with
important titles and distinctive decorated costumes. (From the*
Codex Mendoza)

MAKING A LIVING

In Aztec society there were many different ways to make a living. Even though individuals might not have many choices, the society supported many occupations, from farming the land to making feathered shields to serving the gods.

Farming was the basic occupation of most of the people in the Aztec Empire. They cultivated maize, chiles, beans, squashes, and a variety of vegetables and herbs. Some of these crops required specific environmental conditions. For example, maguey grew in the temperate and cold lands, and cotton and the cacao tree grew in the hot lands. Maize was the most important of the foods that were grown.

The Aztecs worshiped a maize goddess and performed special rituals to help the maize plants grow. Some of these were public ceremonies at which the ruler gave out tamales to everyone in the crowd. Others were more private rituals performed by an individual farmer to ensure the bounty of his family's fields. Even today Aztec descendants in the town of Tepoztlan speak to the seed before planting it, saying,

"My beloved body and strength, go and bear the cold and the storm of the seasons; all is for us."

An Aztec farmer usually produced or collected more than one type of food. Maize farmers, for example, would grow other crops in their fields as well. In the off-season they might hunt rabbits or deer and gather herbs for their own use and to sell in the marketplace. They might also raise dogs and turkeys. Those who cultivated the highly productive chinampas might, in successive seasons, grow maize, then tomatoes, and then flowers, which were required for major ceremonies. Those who fished might also hunt lake birds (especially at the time when ducks migrated to the lakes in huge numbers), transport building materials or travelers in their canoes, and collect lakeside reeds for making mats or baskets.

Whether the men of a household were farmers or fishermen, most produced more than they themselves needed. They used their surplus to pay taxes, buy needed goods in the marketplaces, and to make offerings to the gods. To increase their income and pay

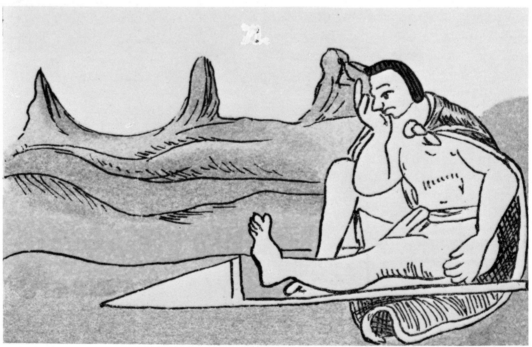

The "good" farmer (top) was hardworking and productive. The "bad" farmer (bottom) was lazy and sure to end in ruin. (From the Florentine Codex)

for the extra goods, Aztec households normally also produced some craft goods, especially cloth, which could be sold in the marketplace.

All Aztec women were expected to produce cloth from wild yucca and maguey or imported cotton as a lifetime occupation. They usually did this at home rather than in workshops (although priestesses also wove in temples). They combined this activity with their other household work, such as marketing, cooking, cleaning, and raising children. The Aztec women were skilled and dedicated weavers who not only produced enough cloth for their own households but also sent surpluses as tribute to the rulers of the Triple Alliance cities. The women of the empire created more than 200,000 items of clothing in a single year to send to the rulers.

Men and women made many other products in the home, such as mats and baskets for sleeping and sitting. They also crafted pottery for cooking and carrying items; gourd bowls (made from a pumpkinlike plant related to the squash); obsidian (volcanic glass) tools; and many other items. Some people were specialists, devoting most of their time and skill to producing a particular item and selling it in marketplaces for other needed goods, including maize.

The fine, artistic creations of the metalworkers, stoneworkers, and featherworkers were especially valued in Aztec society. The fine objects these people produced could be used only by the no-

Dedication stone for the 1487 renovation of the Great Temple at Tenochtitlan, carved from serpentine (green mottled stone). Images of the rulers Tizoc (1481–86) and Ahuitzotl (1486–1502) are carved into the top section of the stone and the date Eight Acatl (1487) is carved into the bottom section. Aztec artisans spent hours crafting jewelry, headdresses, and stones such as these.

bility. In Mexica lore, the god Quetzalcoatl (Ke-tsal-KO-atl), patron god of the Toltecs of Tollan, originated these luxury crafts. The Toltecs were so greatly admired by the Mexica that their name—toltecah—was given to the master artisans.

Carved image of a reclining jaguar from the 15th century. The statue is very naturalistic in style; a characteristic of some Aztec animal sculpture. Even the underside is carved and includes paw pads.

The metalworkers created beautiful jewelry, statues, and gold adornments for the gods. They fashioned copper into jewelry as well as into needles and fishhooks. The stoneworkers polished jade to make necklaces and nose plugs and labored over detailed mosaic pieces of turquoise, dark stones, and pearly shell fragments.

The featherworkers, or *amantecah*, made the most luxurious articles of all. They worked long, painstaking hours designing and then gluing and tying feathers to fashion shields, head-dresses, fans, and other objects. Some of these were made of turkey or duck feathers, but the very finest were made of bright, colorful feathers from tropical birds such as the parrot and macaw. The most prized feathers were those of the *quetzal* (KE-tsal) bird. These feathers were so highly valued that it was forbidden by law to kill the quetzals, and only a few of the long green feathers could be plucked before the bird was released. Because tropical feathers, fine stones, gold, and copper were not found naturally in the Valley of Mexico, the master artisans of the Triple Alliance cities had to rely on the professional merchants and tribute payments from parts of the empire to supply them with these needed raw materials.

The wealthiest pochtecah traded in slaves and fine cotton cloth. Others traded precious metals, stones, and feathers. Although someone could gain a great deal of wealth in this occupation, the risks were also very high because of the travel involved. The merchants traveled to all corners of the empire and beyond its borders as well—as far as Xicalanco on the Gulf Coast and Xoconochco on the Pacific Coast. According to Sahagún, before a young merchant went off to distant parts, he was warned by his elders that he

must first feel and profit by the pain, the afflictions, the privations, the ambushes. Such is exacted from those who go from city to city. . . . Thou shalt be in danger. . . . Thou shalt be long-suffering; thou shalt shed tears. Thy good deeds will not bear fruit, for fatigue will take thy measure.

Pochtecah sometimes served as spies by reporting to their rulers what they saw and heard in marketplaces. They often carried a ruler's goods with them for trade with a distant ruler. This helped set up political ties, but because they were often associated with the imperial rulers, the pochtecah were also feared and sometimes hated by conquered or threatened peoples. They

were sometimes killed and robbed on the road. When this happened the Aztec armies usually took quick revenge.

The pochtecah traveled the greatest distances, traded the most expensive goods, and sometimes served the state, but they were not the only traders in Aztec Mexico. Virtually anyone, from small-scale producers of food or goods to large-scale professional merchants, could trade in the many marketplaces.

The central Mexican marketplace, or *tianquiztli* (tee-an-KEES-tlee), was probably the liveliest spot in any community. There people from all segments of society gathered daily (or in some communities, every five days) to enjoy the company of friends, haggle over prices, and hear and spread the latest news and rumors. The marketplace was usu-

A headdress of Motecuhzoma's made of bright green quetzal feathers and gold ornaments. Featherworkers crafted the most luxurious items in Aztec society.

ally in a large open plaza near a major temple. The grandest plaza of all was at Tlatelolco. The sight of this marketplace so amazed the Spanish soldier Díaz del Castillo that he later wrote:

> After having examined and considered all that we had seen we turned to look at the great market place and the crowds of people that were in it, some buying and others selling, so that the murmur and hum of their voices and words that they used could be heard more than a league [three miles] off. Some of the soldiers among us who had been in many parts of the world, in Constantinople, and all over Italy, and in Rome, said that so large a market place and so full of people, and so well regulated and arranged, they had never beheld before.

As in present-day marketplaces in Mexico, the merchandise was arranged in an orderly way, with vegetables in one area, cloth in another, pottery in yet another, and other items arranged in their respective areas of the marketplace. Buyers and sellers bargained over prices. Much of the buying and selling was done by barter, the exchange of one item for another without the use of money. People brought with them small or large surpluses of goods to exchange. However, some forms of money were used throughout Mexico. Cacao beans and cotton cloth were used as currency. Cacao seems to have been the most common form of money (and

it did, indeed, grow on trees). Although cacao may have served as "small change," it was important enough to lead some people to counterfeit it by removing the beans from the pods, taking out the meat from each bean and refilling it with earth.

Virtually every product of the realm could be found in the major marketplaces. Some people offered services instead of merchandise. One could find barbers, carpenters, and porters at the markets. Many other people in Aztec society made their living by offering services of one kind or another. Rulers and other government officials, judges, and warriors served the state, and priests served the gods. Scribes, astrologers, midwives, physicians, and entertainers were all highly trained in their specialties and served others in the Aztec communities.

There were many Aztec government officials. Of the Mexica alone, Father Durán commented in the 16th century that "the nation had a special official for every activity, small though it were. Everything was so well recorded that no detail was left out of the accounts. There were even officials in charge of sweeping."

The enormous empire of the Aztecs required a large and complex government. Eventually the Mexica and their allies controlled most of central and southern Mexico. This vast region was made up of many city-states.

Over the course of its imperial history, from 1430 to 1521, the Aztec Empire had eight official rulers, or

MEXICA RULERS

Ruler	Meaning of Name	Name Glyph	Dates of Reign
Acamapichtli (A-ka-ma-PEECH-tlee)	Handful of Reeds		1372–1391
Huitzilihuitl (Wee-tsee-LEE-weetl)	Hummingbird Feather		1391–1415
Chimalpopoca (Chee-mal-po-PO-ka)	Smoking Shield		1415–1426
Itzcoatl (Eets-KO-atl)	Obsidian Serpent		1426–1440
Motecuhzoma Ilhuicamina (Mo-tek'w-SO-ma Eel-wee-ka-MEE-na)	Angry Lord, Archer of the Skies		1440–1468
Axayacatl (A-sha-YA-katl)	Face of Water		1468–1481
Tizoc (TEE-sok)	Bloodletter		1481–1486
Ahuitzotl (A-WEE-tsotl)	A water animal		1486–1502
Motecuhzoma Xocoyotzin (Mo-tek-'w-SO-ma Sho-ko-YO-tsin)	Angry Lord, the Younger		1502–1520

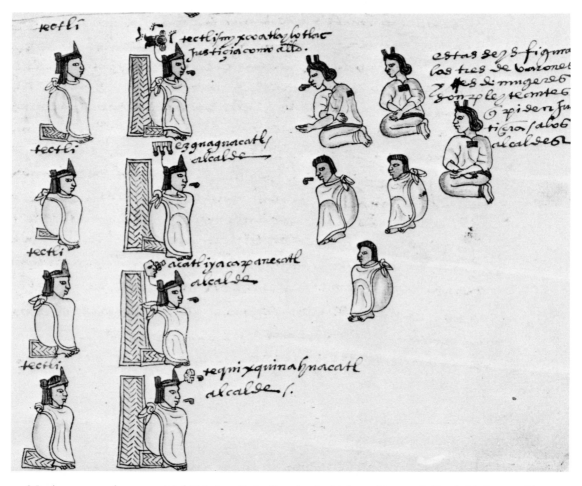

Mexica men and women (right) *bring their disputes to high-ranking and* (far left) *low-ranking judges, who will listen and then pass judgment. (From the* Codex Mendoza)

tlatoque. Each new personality brought a different manner and degree of strength to the office of ruler. Ahuitzotl (1486–1502) was, at least outwardly, generous and loving to his people; Tizoc (1481–86) was, by contrast, weak and less than courageous on the battlefield. (His early death may not have been an accident.) Motecuhzoma Xocoyotzin, who ruled from 1502 until his death in 1520, was serious and severe, feared rather than loved by his subjects.

The types of activities undertaken by the people of a city-state could be influenced by the preferences of their ruler. The Mexica ruler Motecuhzoma Ilhuicamina especially encouraged military might and conquest, and the Aztec Empire grew enormously during his rule, from 1440–68. His contemporary at Texcoco, Nezahualcoyotl (1418–72), favored law, engineering, and the arts. It was partly a consequence of their rulers' interests that by the 16th century the city of Tenochtitlan had become the military leader of the Triple Alliance, and Texcoco the seat of the highest court and the center of artistic activity.

There were many other governing positions below the tlatoani. The ruler was assisted in his decisions by a vice-ruler or Cihuacoatl (See-wa-KO-atl: Woman Serpent); a Council of Four (an advisory group normally made up of close relatives); and a supreme council of 12 to 20 nobles. While the ruler was busy making wars and alliances, the vice-ruler took care of the day-to-day management of the details of government.

Each city-state had a multilevel court system that employed many judges. The state appointed the judges who heard cases. The highest court in the land heard cases brought by nobles. The lowest courts were at the calpulli level. Sahagún described the judicial process for cases involving commoners:

> Every day the common folk and vassals laid complaints before [the judges]. Calmly and prudently they heard the plaints of the vassals; in the picture writing which recorded the cases, they studied the complaints. And when they tested their truth, they sought out and inquired of informers and witnesses who could size up the plaintiffs, [who knew] what had been stolen and what was charged.

Serious cases involving commoners and nobles alike went to the higher courts.

For both nobles and commoners, justice was swift and punishment severe. Theft, homicide, and public drunkenness were considered serious crimes. Individuals caught stealing might be placed in slavery to the person from whom they stole. The act of homicide normally carried a penalty of slavery or death. Drunkenness was believed to cause such problems as poverty, boasting, quarreling, and stealing and was therefore severely punished. Records show that priests or government officials could suffer the death penalty for being drunk in public, but commoners would be punished by having their head shaved in public and their house destroyed. In general, it was common for nobles to be punished more severely than commoners for similar crimes.

In matters of warfare, the ruler was advised by a war council made up of all warriors entitled to be called "seasoned warrior" because they had captured at least four enemy warriors in battle. The war council met in a room of the royal palace to discuss future war campaigns and offered military advice to the ruler. Because there was no large-scale standing army among the Aztecs, most warriors were commoners who were trained in military skills but who spent most of their time farming, fishing, or toiling in another occupation; however, there were professional military men, generals and other officers and members of the knightly orders.

Each god, goddess, and temple had its own group of priests and/or priestesses who were trained from an early age in temple schools for a religious life. Priests spent much of their time maintaining the temples. They swept the floors, cared for the sculpture of the god and the deity's accoutrements, such as clothing and banners. They attended to any additions or repairs to the temple itself. They also participated in an endless round of rituals, offering penances, prayers, and incense and were responsible for the education of the sons of nobles in the temple schools. These daily activities were interrupted by important events, such as major rituals, or a war, in which priests would join in battle. The duties of priestesses were confined more to the temples, where they would sweep, offer incense, organize ceremonies, and weave and embroider fine cloth to adorn the sculptures of their gods and goddesses.

Scribes had an important role in Aztec society. They produced extensive manuscripts, known as *codices*, written in picture symbols. These contained all the official records of the empire: descriptions of religious ceremonies, schedules of government events, names of rulers, tribute payments, histories of migrations and conquests, maps, censuses, and legal decisions. These books were housed in huge libraries. The scribes wrote down in a codex only the most outstanding features of an event to serve as a reminder; the details were stored in the memory of the writer and reader. (Some codices survive and are often known by the name of the library that owns them or of a person or place associated with them in some way.) The scribes were a highly skilled and well-educated group.

Becoming an astrologer also required a long and thorough education. Virtually everyone called upon these specialists at some point in their lives. Astrologers helped at an infant's naming ceremony, set the date for a marriage, fixed a proper day for a merchant's feast, and even selected the best day to begin a war.

Midwives and physicians (often women) were also extremely knowledgeable, especially in the use of herbs, splints, and other cures. They usually learned their profession from a close relative or associate.

Entertainers, such as musicians and jugglers, required training and development of their skills. These people often performed at feasts.

There was a category of people who served as unskilled laborers. Among them were porters. These laborers were important in Aztec society because all goods could be transported only by canoe or on human backs. Porters were numerous and important in moving large quantities of materials from city to city, mountain to valley, or Triple Alliance capital to foreign trading center. There were also those who lived by gambling. But the Aztecs felt that anyone following that path would surely end in ruin.

The Mexica worked hard, but they also played. Their most popular games

An Aztec herbal explains the use of the Mexican plant Tonatinh yxiuh ahhuachcho, *or Sun's Herb (of the dew) to treat "spongy swellings." The manuscript was compiled in Nahuatl by Martín de la Cruz, and translated into Latin by Juan Badiano (both Indian scholars) in 1552 soon after the original compilation. (From the* Badianas Herbal)

were a ball game called *tlachtli* (TLACH-tlee) and a game of chance called *patolli* (pa-TO-lee). The ball game was played for entertainment, gambling, and divination (attempts to obtain knowledge of unknown present or future events). The ball court, which can be seen today at many archaeological sites dating from A.D. 300 to A.D. 1200, was 100 to 200 feet (330 to 660 meters) long and constructed in the shape of an *I*. It was surrounded by high walls and usually had a doughnut-shaped ring set perpendicular to the ground into the mid-

point of the two longer walls of the court. The game was played with a hard rubber ball, which the players hit back and forth with some part of their body other than their hands; use of the hands was a foul. Fouls were also counted if the ball was hit into a team's backcourt, or if a team failed to return the ball. Apparently, a team that managed to hit the ball through the ring won.

The game was quite lively and rough, and players were quick and skillful. It was wise (even necessary) for the players' bodies to be protected with

A favorite game of the Mexica was patolli. *Four beans were tossed, much as we use dice, and stones were moved along a marked board. Rich feathers and fine stone jewelry were wagered on the game. It was overseen by the patron god, Macuilxochitl (Five Flower). (From the* Codex Magliabechiano)

gloves, girdles, and hip guards made of deerskin. Even so, players could be badly bruised, and sometimes even fatally injured, if they were hit by a ball.

Tlachtli provided an occasion for much gambling. People wagered everything from precious stones to clothing, feathers, houses, fields, and slaves. In the 16th century, Father Durán learned that some people had gambled away "their fields, their corn granaries, their maguey plants. They sold their children in order to bet and even staked themselves and became slaves." Sometimes the ball game was played strictly for entertainment and gambling, but it was also played to help a ruler predict the outcome of a war or to make any major decision.

Patolli was much like present-day Parcheesi. It was played on a board or marked surface such as a mat with counters made of pebbles. Dried beans, marked with white dots to indicate numbers, were used much as we use dice. Each player moved six counters on the board according to throws of the beans. Some people became very attached to the game and to the gambling that often accompanied it. According to Durán,

the gamblers dedicated to this game always went about with the mats under their armpits and with the dice tied up in small cloths. . . . It was believed that they [the dice] were mighty. . . . They spoke to them and begged them to be favorable, to come to their aid in that game.

Aside from these entertainments, the daily routines were often interrupted by special events, public duties, and religious ceremonies. Special events took place when a new temple was dedicated, warriors returned from battle, a ruler died, or a new ruler was installed. Public duties, performed mostly by men, included work on special projects such as building roads or temples or marching to war. Some religious ceremonies involved only the priests in their temples, who fasted, feasted, and made offerings (including sacrifices). Some religious ceremonies were large, splendid affairs, involving the entire community in fasting, dancing, singing, making offerings, and watching or participating in dazzling processions.

Still other ceremonies were those of the household that involved few people but marked the most important events in a person's life. These were birth and the naming of an infant, entering and leaving the formal schools, marriage, and death. ▲

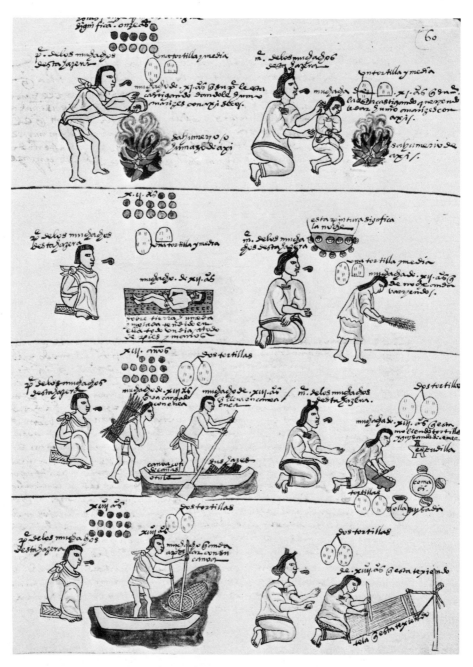

Episodes in the education of boys, (left) and girls, (right). At the top, 11-year-olds are punished by being held next to burning chiles. In the second row, a father lectures his 12-year-old son on the exemplary life, and a girl sweeps. In the third row, 13-year-old boys begin adult work carrying goods on foot and by canoe, while a girl learns to cook. At the bottom, a father teaches his 14-year-old son to fish and a mother teaches her daughter to weave. (From the Codex Mendoza.*)*

LIFE CYCLE
AND
EDUCATION

From birth to death, ceremonies guided the lives of the Mexica. When a baby was born, the midwife who assisted with the birth had to dispose of the umbilical cord in a ceremonial way: It was buried by the hearth if the baby were a girl or carried to a field of battle if a boy. Each place symbolized the infant's future. A girl's lifework would tie her to the home and a boy's fate would probably lead him to the battlefield.

Shortly after a baby was born, an astrologer was called in to read the child's fate in the "book of days," or *tonalamatl* (to-nal-A-matl). The Mexica believed that a person's future was determined by the gods and the stars. The course of an entire life depended on the person's date and time of birth. These readings would predict whether the child would become wealthy or poor, honorable or dishonorable. Some days were considered "good" and others "bad." For example, only weakness and bad temper were associated with the day the Mexica called Six Dog. If a child were born on such an especially bad day, the astrologer would suggest

that the bathing and naming ceremony be held on a more favorable day. In this case, the next day, known as Seven Monkey, would have been a good choice because persons born under that sign were destined to be cheerful, respected, and wealthy.

At the bathing ceremony, the midwife bathed the infant and presented it with miniature tools that symbolized its future duties. A boy was given a small shield, a bow, four arrows, and a cloak and loincloth. A girl was given spinning and weaving tools and a tunic and skirt, which women wore everywhere. The infant was then named and dressed. Older children then went running off, shouting the new name for all to hear. The family enjoyed a great feast prepared by the women.

Children were often named for the day of their birth. This resulted in names such as Ce Coatl (One Snake), Macuilli Tochtli (Five Rabbit) or Ome Mazatl (Two Deer). But other names were also given. A girl might be named Quiauhxochitl (Kee-ow-SHO-cheetl), "Rain Flower," and a boy might be

A mother and her baby consult an astrologer. Soon after birth, an astrologer was called in to select an appropriate day for naming the baby. (From the Florentine Codex)

named Itzcoatl (Eets-KO-atl), "Obsidian Snake." When the Spanish friars arrived in Mexico, they baptized many Indians and gave each a Christian name, but the Indians usually kept at least part of their original name as a surname. This practice produced names such as Juan Icnoyotl (John Misery) and Pedro Tochtli (Peter Rabbit).

Little was expected of young children. However, as they grew, they were taught the rules of the exemplary life and helped with household chores. By age 5 boys were carrying firewood, and by age 14 they were able to fish in the lake from a canoe. At age 6 a girl was taught to spin, and by age 14 she could also weave and cook. Children were taught to be hardworking, moderate, and humble. Punishments were often severe if they did not improve their behavior after being reprimanded.

The mildest form of punishment was scolding. According to Sahagún a child might be scolded by comparing him with an Otomí, a neighboring people held in very low regard by the Mexica:

Now thou art an Otomí. Now thou art a miserable Otomí. O Otomí, how is it that thou understandest not? Art thou per chance a real Otomí? Not only art thou like an Otomí, thou art a real Otomí, a miserable Otomí, a green-head, a thick-head, a big tuft of hair over the back of the head, an Otomí blockhead.

(continued on page 73)

ART OF THE AZTEC EMPIRE

The great civilization of the Aztecs produced beautiful works of art, some powerful and some delicate. During the height of the empire, from 1430 to 1519, their artisans crafted sophisticated sculptures, mosaics, featherwork, and gold jewelry. The Aztecs worked a great deal in stone, both dark volcanic stones such as basalt and semiprecious stones such as crystal, jadeite, and turquoise. Some of the most familiar Aztec images are the monumental stone figures of gods and goddesses, but perhaps their finest works are the delicate stone and feather mosaics and gold jewelry. Many impressive artifacts have been unearthed during excavations of Huey Teocalli, or the Great Temple, of Tenochtitlan. Some of these dramatic objects can be seen today in the Museum of Anthropology in Mexico City.

An excavation site at the Great Temple of Tenochtitlan. Shells, clay masks, bowls, and other objects in this pit were offerings to the gods. The remains of the temple were found beneath present-day Mexico City. Excavations took place in the late 1970s and early 1980s.

*A panel of skulls from an altar on the north side of the Great
Temple. Three of the altar's sides are covered with these
stylized skulls sculpted of stone and covered with stucco. The
panel represents the skull racks, or tzompantli, on which the
heads of those sacrificed to the gods were displayed.*

Symbols of death, such as skulls, were common motifs in Aztec art. **Left:** A human skull decorated with a mosaic of turquoise, iron pyrite, and shell. The Aztecs' preoccupation with death was intertwined with their belief that death was necessary for the creation of life.

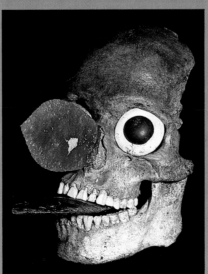

A human skull excavated from the Great Temple. Stone knives and eyes were inserted in the skull before it was offered to the gods.

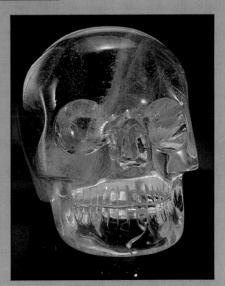

This skull, measuring less than 4 inches in height, was sculpted from a piece of crystal, a glasslike quartz.

This gold nose ornament in the shape of a stylized butterfly (about 3 inches high) was found at the foot of a stairway in the area of the Great Temple.

Gold hummingbird ear ornaments (2 1/2 inches long) from Oaxaca, in a part of the Aztec Empire southeast of Tenochtitlan.

A two-headed serpent of turquoise and shell mosaic (about 16 inches long). Unlike the gold ornaments at left, which may have adorned statues of gods or goddesses, this piece may have been worn as a pendant by a powerful noble. To make mosaics, stoneworkers cut small pieces of jade, crystal, pyrite, shell, and turquoise, and fitted them into knife handles, helmets, shields, and skulls.

69

Jadeite (a type of jade) mask (about 6 inches wide) of the moon-goddess Coyolxauhqui. This mask was probably worn across the chest of a priest on special occasions. The most skilled artisans spent much of their time producing objects relating to the gods, goddesses, and rituals of the Aztec religion.

A **chacmool,** *a reclining figure holding a container for the hearts of persons sacrificed to the gods from the Great Temple.*

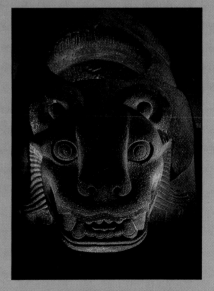

A mask on a ceramic vessel offered at the Great Temple. The strips that outline the eyes are characteristic of the rain-god Tlaloc.

This crouching stone jaguar, or **ocelocuauhxicalli** *(about 7 feet long), served as a receptacle for the hearts of sacrificed persons.*

This life-size ceramic eagle warrior was one of a pair flanking a doorway to the chamber where the eagle warriors met near the Great Temple. The eagle was a representation of the sun.

A painted stone sculpture, from the Great Temple area, of the god of pulque (a fermented drink).

Fathers taught their sons specialized crafts in the home. Here sons are learning (clockwise from top left) *carpentry, stonework, metalwork, and painting. (From the* Codex Mendoza)

(continued from page 64)

If scolding failed to correct the child's behavior, more direct measures were used. The child might be beaten with a stick, pierced with maguey spines, or held over the painful fumes of burning chiles.

All of this moral and practical education took place within the household. But education outside the home was also required. Historical records indicate that boys and girls between the ages of 12 and 15 attended a House of Song, or *cuicacalli* (kwee-ka-KA-lee), in the evenings. These schools were lo-

cated next to the temples. Here the young people learned how to sing, dance, and play musical instruments such as drums and wind instruments. This instruction was essential because song and dance were important parts of religious ceremonies. Songs also taught the children about the Mexica views of creation, life and death, and the gods.

All noble boys started their formal education by age 15. They entered a school called the *calmecac* (kal-ME-kak). These schools were associated with temples and run by priests. The boys were kept very busy with both physical work and studies. Typically, they would arise before dawn and sweep the temple or go to the nearby hills to collect maguey thorns, which were used for rituals, or firewood. During the day they worked at cultivating fields, building canals, or making adobe bricks for the construction and repair of public buildings. At some point in the afternoon, they would worship their gods and study history, writing, the calendars, and the law. They also learned military arts. The priests of the calmecac performed ceremonies many times during the night, and the young men participated in some of these.

Formal education was also required for boys of commoner background. By age 15, a boy entered the *telpochcalli* (telpoch-KA-lee) of his district. Here he worked and slept and was instructed in the military arts. These boys also spent a great deal of time at hard physical labor: cultivating crops, digging canals, or constructing buildings.

A girl's education took place primarily in the home, although she might spend a year of service in a temple when she was 12 or 13 years old. Some girls later dedicated themselves to the priesthood. Most girls were probably ready to marry by age 15.

Whether of noble or common class, most boys left their schools by age 20 and were ready for marriage. Arranging a marriage was an elaborate and time-consuming business for the Mexica. Elderly female matchmakers were em-

A terra-cotta figure of a mother and child expresses the importance of motherhood.

ployed by the parents of a boy and they would discuss marriage with the parents of a particular girl. After an arrangement was made, astrologers were consulted to set a wedding date, and many feasts were given by the parents of the young couple slated to be married. Finally, a great feast, as grand as the bride's parents could afford, was prepared. Sahagún recorded that ground cacao was prepared, flowers were secured, smoking tubes were purchased, tubes of tobacco were prepared, sauce bowls and pottery cups and baskets were purchased. Then maize was ground. . . . Then tamales were prepared . . . perhaps three days or two days the women made tamales.

After the feasting, the bride was decorated with feathers, and parts of her body were painted. She was lectured by the elders of her household about her role as wife and future mother, and then she was carried to the groom's house. Here, the matchmakers tied the couple together by their clothing, literally "tying the knot."

With marriage bonds established, the young couple took on adult responsibilities. They established a household, raised children, and worked at the occupations for which they had been trained.

Aztec households grew to be large, including not only husband, wife, and children but also frequently in-laws, grandparents, nephews, nieces, and others. The houses of the nobility were generally larger and more elaborate than those of the commoners. One reason for this was wealth itself. Another reason was the practice of *polygyny*, whereby a man has more than one wife. Polygyny was a privilege reserved for nobles and, among the Aztecs, especially the rulers. Such practice could result in enormous households. For example, Nezahualpilli (Ne-sa-wal-

Drunkenness was prohibited in Aztec society because it was considered the root of all evil. The Mexica believed that it might lead one to steal. In this detail from the Codex Mendoza, *stolen goods lie between two drinking Aztecs. The bundle of rope (right) symbolizes pulque, an alcoholic drink. As a privilege of age, elders were allowed to drink to excess.*

PEE-lee), ruler of Texcoco from 1472–1515, is said to have had more than 2,000 wives and 144 children. Only 11 of his children were considered legitimate, but the others nonetheless inherited great wealth and important titles. This ruler's father, Nezahualcoyotl (Ne-sa-wal-KO-yotl), apparently fathered 60 sons and 57 daughters. Aside from producing a great number of heirs, polygyny provided a way for rulers and high-ranking nobles to make political alliances with their neighbors. By marrying several high-ranking noblewomen, a ruler or nobleman established friendly political ties.

With the arrival of old age, a Mexica became a respected elder. Sahagún wrote that "the good old man [is] famous, honored, an advisor . . . a counselor, an indoctrinator. He tells, he

A deceased merchant is wrapped in cloth in a mummy bundle (left center), *surrounded by his possessions—including feathers, jade, gold, and a jaguar skin—and prepared for his journey through the underworld. (From the* Codex Magliabechiano)

relates ancient lore; he leads an exemplary life." The respected old woman was "one who never abandons the house . . . a supervisor, a manager, a shelter."

Elders were expected to instruct the young, but not all elders took this responsibility seriously. The "bad old man," for example, was "an old fool, a liar. He invents falsehoods," according to Sahagún. Good or bad, elderly men and women had special privileges in Aztec society. One of these was the right to drink heavily in public. Drunkenness was strongly prohibited in Mex-

ica culture, but those over 70 years of age were allowed this privilege. The Aztecs drank pulque, made from the fermented juices of the maguey root.

Some Mexica lived for many years. Others died young by falling in battle, being sacrificed, or as a result of serious accident or illness. The Mexica believed that the future of a person in the afterworld depended on the manner in which he or she died rather than on the kind of life the person had led. For instance, one who died in the realm of the water gods—by drowning or by being struck by lightning—would have a happy afterlife, forever at ease in beautiful green gardens. A woman who died in childbirth was considered comparable to a warrior who lost his life on the battlefield, and each would have a glorious afterlife.

The women who died in childbirth were believed to be responsible for carrying the sun from its zenith (its highest point in the sky) to its setting. At sunset, these women roamed about the earth as *cihuateteo* (see-wa-te-TE-o), goddesses who might suddenly appear at a crossroads and frighten and cause bodily harm to a person. Warriors who died in battle or on the sacrificial stone traveled with the sun each day on its journey from its rising to the zenith. After spending four years in this fashion, they returned to earth as hummingbirds or butterflies.

Most people, however, descended to the world of Mictlan (MEEK-tlan) when they died. The Mexica believed this underworld was a place of eternal, dark emptiness that had nine levels. The deceased had to travel through each in turn, assisted by the possessions that had been buried with them. If possible, plenty of food and a yellow dog were also included in the burial. The journey took four years. It could be made easier by the living, who could make offerings on the person's behalf during that time. The deceased traveled through mountains, past a serpent and a green lizard, across eight deserts, over eight hills, through the painful "place of the obsidian-bladed winds," and across the "place of the nine rivers" to arrive finally at the deepest layer of the underworld.

Those who had followed the exemplary life were generally given funerals with all the proper rituals and plenty of food and other goods to assist in their journey. They also were remembered by the living and aided by their occasional offerings. Those who had lived less-than-ideal lives were more likely to suffer on their journey through the underworld because they would probably receive less protection and assistance, such as being shielded from the obsidian-bladed winds or receiving assistance from the yellow dog. This was one motivation for living Mexica to conform to the rules of behavior during the time that they were living on the earth. ▲

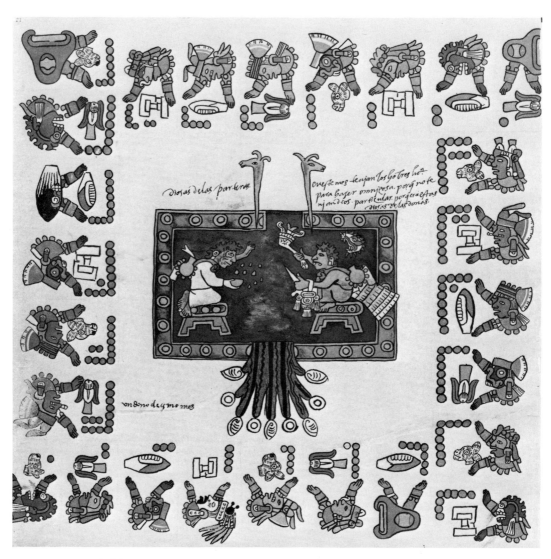

A folio from the Codex Borbonicus shows the creator god and
goddess, Ometecuhtli and Omecihuatl, from whom all life and
sustenance come. The border is made up of calendar symbols
recording the passage of time.

BELIEFS
AND
GODS

The Mexica worshiped many gods who influenced their lives and created their world. According to their beliefs, the universe was created by two of these gods, Ometecuhtli, "Lord of Duality" and Omecihuatl, "Lady of Duality." These gods had four sons, two of whom were responsible for further creation, including the creation of more gods, humans, other living creatures, and environments.

This creative process lasted for four ages, or "suns," until the current sun appeared. Each of the first four suns was destroyed by a catastrophic event, such as a great flood or hurricanes. After each destruction the world had to be created anew. The current, or fifth, age is ruled by the sun god Tonatiuh (To-na-TEE-yooh). An image of this god may appear in the center of the Aztec calendar stone. According to Mexica beliefs, this age is eventually to be destroyed by earthquakes.

To help prevent the destruction of the fifth sun, the Mexica celebrated the new fire ceremony. This solemn and tense religious event was held every 52 years. On the designated day, the

people extinguished all fires and discarded most of their belongings, such as their household idols (figures or statues representing gods), cooking implements, and hearthstones. They carefully swept and cleaned their houses, inside and out. At dusk, everyone climbed on top of houses and walls. Pregnant women had to cover their faces with maguey-leaf masks. Children were similarly protected and required to stay alert because it was believed that unmasked or sleeping children would be turned into mice.

During the night, priests climbed a hill near Tenochtitlan and, exactly at midnight, sacrificed a man by cutting out his heart. Then they kindled the "new fire" in the chest cavity of the sacrificed captive. If the fire flamed up, it was a sign that the universe would continue for another 52 years. This fire lit torches carried by the fastest runners to light all the torches and hearths at temples, schools, and houses. If a fire could not be kindled, it was a signal that the world of the fifth sun would come to an end. The earth would become completely dark and *tzitzimime* (tsee-

The Stone of the Five Suns is carved with symbols for seven dates in the Aztec calendar system. Five of these are the termination dates of the five ages, or "suns," into which the Aztecs divided the history of the universe: 4 Jaguar (lower right), 4 Wind (upper right), 4 Rain (upper left), 4 Water (lower left), and 4 Movement (center).

tsee-MEE-me), monsters from the heavens, would come and devour all human beings.

This ritual, which took place with the entire population looking on anxiously, highlights several important Aztec beliefs. The Mexica and their neighbors believed, first, that time was cyclical. Each cycle was made up of 52 years, and their people were forever moving through 52-year periods. This

concept provided the mythological basis for the new fire ceremony. They also felt that they lived in a world of uncertainty, ruled by the gods and fate. But at the same time, they felt that they could influence their destiny and that they actually had an obligation to do so. This is why they refused to stand by and let the sun be destroyed but rather took an active part in trying to keep the present world intact.

Over time, the Mexica adopted the gods of their neighbors. By the time Cortés arrived, the Mexica and their neighbors had developed an extensive pantheon. Some Aztec gods were orig-

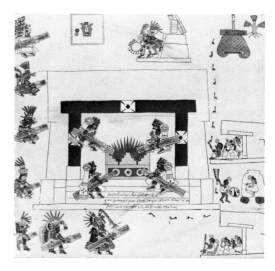

The new fire ceremony, which was held every 52 years. Priests carried torches, which would be lit by the new fire and used to light all of the new fires in the land. Children and pregnant women (right) were required to cover their face with a mask during the ceremony. (From the Codex Borbonicus)

Name of Sun	Presiding Deity	Human Population	Age Ends in Destruction by:	Fate of Humanity
1. Four Jaguar (*Nahui Ocelotl*)	Tezcatlipoca ("Smoking Mirror")	Giants living on acorns	Jaguars	Eaten by jaguars
2. Four Wind (*Nahui Ehecatl*)	Quetzalcoatl (God of Wind and Air)	Humans living on piñon nuts	Hurricanes	Changed into monkeys
3. Four Rain (*Nahui Quiahuitl*)	Tlaloc (Rain God)	Humans living on aquatic seeds	Fiery rain	Changed into dogs, turkeys, and butterflies
4. Four Water (*Nahui Atl*)	Chalchiuhtlicue (Water Goddess)	Humans living on wild seeds, probably a wild ancestor of maize	Great flood	Changed into fish
5. Four Movement (*Nahui Ollin*)	Tonatiuh (Sun God)	Humans living on maize	Earthquakes	To be destroyed by *tzitzimime* (celestial monsters)

inally Chichimec gods, others came from the early settled civilizations in the Valley of Mexico, and some were from their allies and enemies. As a symbol of conquest, the Mexica would burn an enemy's temple and then take the temple god's idol to Tenochtitlan, thereby absorbing it into their culture.

Each god was connected with some aspect of the universe. Some gods related to the abstract and philosophical aspects of the world. The Lord and Lady of Duality were included in this group, as was Tezcatlipoca (Tes-ka-tlee-PO-ka), "Smoking Mirror." He had extensive powers because with his mirror he could see everything. However, he was especially concerned with warfare and wizardry.

Many more gods, however, were concerned with rain and fertility. Tlaloc, the major fertility god, was extremely important to all central Mexicans. Sahagún recorded that

> to him was attributed the rain; for he made it, he caused it to come down, he scattered the rain like seed, and

The goddess Tlazolteotl giving birth to the god of corn. This goddess was known as the "eater of filth," and the Mexica confessed their wrongs to her. She is considered one of the mother goddesses. The sculpture is carved from green aplite, a type of granite.

also the hail. He caused to sprout, to blossom, to leaf out, to bloom, to ripen, the trees, the plants, our food. And also by him were made floods of water and thunder-bolts.

Because of his importance, Tlaloc shared the great temple of Tenochtitlan with Huitzilopochtli, the Mexica patron god.

The goddess Chalchiuhtlicue (Chal-chee-uh-TLEE-kwe), "Jade-Her-Skirt,"

also controlled the forces of water. Toci (TO-see), "Our Grandmother," was a mother goddess. Another of these, Tonantzin (To-NAN-tseen), "Our Revered Mother," later became associated with the Virgin Mary after the Indians were introduced to Christianity.

There were also many gods and goddesses responsible for the maize plant. Quetzalcoatl, one of the oldest and most celebrated of the Aztec gods, was one of these. He was worshiped in rituals throughout central and southern Mexico and was credited with having given maize as well as the fine arts to humans.

Several gods were concerned with warfare, a major activity of the Mexica and their neighbors. Huitzilopochtli, the Mexica's patron god, was a war god. Tonatiuh was the sun god and all warriors were dedicated to his service. Warriors provided the sun with captives for sacrifice. Men who died on the battlefield or in sacrifice joined the sun from dawn until noon on its daily journey.

Some gods served as special patrons or protectors to calpulli, city-states, or craft groups. For instance, midwives especially looked to the goddess Toci, and metalworkers worshiped Xipe Totec (SHEE-pe TO-tek).

Many of the public ceremonies of the Mexica involved human sacrifice. The Mexica believed that they were largely responsible for maintaining the universe and that their success depended on the offering of human blood. Priests frequently offered their

A stone sculpture representing the goddess of water and springs, Chalchiuhtlicue (Jade-Her-Skirt). This figure is seated with her hands on her knees.

The feathered serpent was a symbol of the god Quetzalcoatl. Carved serpents such as this one adorned many temples and walls.

own blood by piercing parts of their body with maguey thorns. At some rituals the entire population pierced themselves. On a larger scale, however, the Mexica and their neighbors offered the hearts of enemy captives or of persons who were given the honor of impersonating gods.

Many Mexica myths provided the basis for the practice of human sacrifice. One was the story of the creation of the fifth sun, which could not be accomplished until a god leaped into a fire and sacrificed himself. (Nanahuatzin [Na-na-WA-tseen] volunteered.) Another myth tells of the birth of Huitzilopochtli, who is considered a sun god in this story. Huitzilopochtli was miraculously conceived when his goddess mother placed a ball of feathers in her belt. Later she learned she was to bear a child. She had already borne a daughter, Coyolxauhqui (Ko-yol-sha-UH-kee), and 400 sons. Her 400 sons represented the stars and her daughter represented the moon. Realizing that this offspring would be different, these children became extremely upset by their mother's latest pregnancy and joined together to attack her. But just

(continued on page 88)

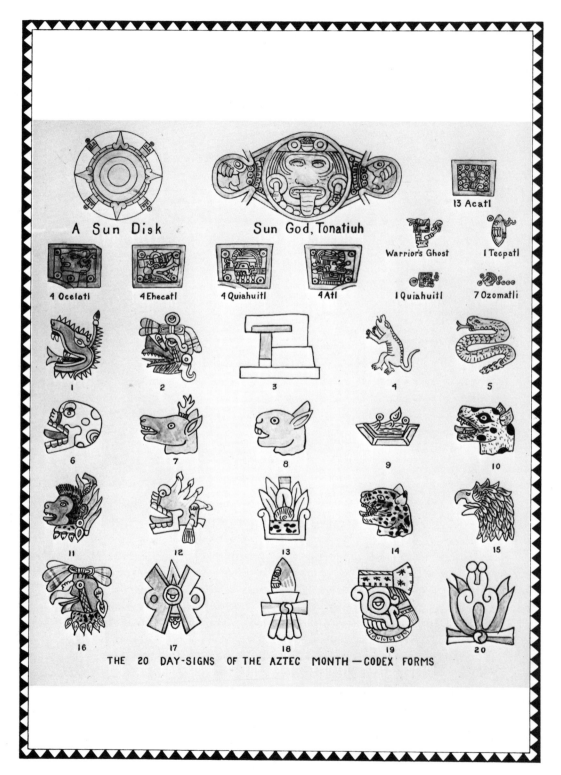

A Sun Disk

Sun God, Tonatiuh

13 Acatl

Warrior's Ghost

1 Tecpatl

4 Ocelotl

4 Ehecatl

4 Quiahuitl

4 Atl

1 Quiahuitl

7 Ozomatli

THE 20 DAY-SIGNS OF THE AZTEC MONTH—CODEX FORMS

TELLING TIME:
THE AZTEC CALENDARS

Aztec life was guided by two interrelated calendars, one solar and the other ritual. The solar calendar consisted of 365 days. It was divided into 18 months of 20 days each, with each month further divided into 4 weeks of 5 days. The remaining five days were added on at the end of the year. These were always considered unlucky days. The solar calendar was tied to the agricultural cycle and was used to set major marketing days, which communities often held once a week.

The ritual calendar was called the *tonalpohualli* (To-nal-po-WAL-lee), or "count of days." The days on this calendar were made up of a sequence of 20 names, such as snake, reed, or rain, with the numbers 1 through 13. Each name was combined with each number to produce 260 days, each known by a unique number-name. The calendar begins with One Alligator and continues with Two Wind, Three House, and so on. After 260 days from the beginning of the count, One Alligator will appear again. The astrologers made particularly important use of this calendar to predict a person's fate or to select especially good days for a big event such as a wedding or the installation of a new ruler. Each number-name combination carried its own special fortune, either a good, bad, or indifferent one.

When both Aztec calendars were combined, they produced a 52-year cycle of 18,980 unique days. For example, Tenochtitlan, the capital of the Aztec Empire, fell to the Spaniards on August 13, 1521. This was the second day of the month of Xocotl Uetzi (SHO-kotl WE-tsee) in the solar calendar and One Snake in the ritual calendar. This particular date, Two Xocotl Uetzi/ One Snake would not reappear for another 52 solar years.

The Aztecs viewed time as cyclical. At the end of every 52-year cycle, special rituals took place to "tie up the years." Bundles of reeds, representing the years, were literally tied up. A new cycle would then begin, without reference to the previous cycle. The particular 52-year cycle in which they were at any given point was not important to the Aztecs because they viewed time as forever moving through these cycles.

TONALPOHUALLI (COUNT OF DAYS) OR RITUAL CALENDAR

Associated Numbers	Day Name Meaning	Glyph	Associated Numbers	Day Name Meaning	Glyph
1, 8, 2, 9 . . .	cipactli (alligator)		11, 5, 12, 6 . . .	ozomatli (monkey)	
2, 9, 3, 10 . . .	ehecatl (wind)		12, 6, 13, 7 . . .	malinalli (grass)	
3, 10, 4, 11 . . .	calli (house)		13, 7, 1, 8 . . .	acatl (reed)	
4, 11, 5, 12 . . .	cuetzpallin (lizard)		1, 8, 2, 9 . . .	ocelotl (jaguar)	
5, 12, 6, 13 . . .	coatl (snake)		2, 9, 3, 10 . . .	cuauhtli (eagle)	
6, 13, 7, 1 . . .	miquiztli (death)		3, 10, 4, 11 . . .	cozcacuauhtli (vulture)	
7, 1, 8, 2 . . .	mazatl (deer)		4, 11, 5, 12 . . .	ollin (movement)	
8, 2, 9, 3 . . .	tochtli (rabbit)		5, 12, 6, 13 . . .	tecpatl (flint knife)	
9, 3, 10, 4 . . .	atl (water)		6, 13, 7, 1 . . .	quiahuitl (rain)	
10, 4, 11, 5 . . .	itzcuintli (dog)		7, 1, 8, 2 . . .	xochitl (flower)	

A solar disk, the calendar of the sun, about 10 feet in diameter, now in the Mexican National Museum of Anthropology in Mexico City. The face of Tonatiuh, the sun deity, is in the center, surrounded by symbols for the worlds that preceded Aztec times. The narrow inner band shows the 20 day signs of the Aztec month.

Human sacrifice being performed by priests on top of an Aztec temple. (From the Codex Magliabechiano)

Volcanic stone statue representing Xipe Totec, "Our Lord the Flayed One," the god of spring, shown as a priest dressed in the skin of a sacrificed person. This type of statue was set up as a standard-bearer outside Aztec temples. The date 1 Acatl (1507) carved into the back of the statue— the year in which the last new fire ceremony was performed in the Aztecs' 52-year calendar—may have been the date the statue was erected.

(continued from page 83)

in time Huitzilopochtli was born, fully armed with a fire serpent, darts, and a shield. He eliminated Coyolxauhqui with the fire serpent and destroyed her 400 brothers with his darts and dart thrower. The Mexica believed that each day this event was reenacted: The sun (Huitzilopochtli) fought the moon and stars for control of the heavens. In order

for each new day to dawn, the Mexica had to help the sun in his battle by providing him with nourishment in the form of human blood.

Most sacrifices were performed by removing the heart, but people dedicated to the rain gods, often children, were sacrificed by drowning. Others might be slain in ritual combat or shot with arrows. These were always ritual deaths. The sacrifices took place in a religious context, only during the most important ceremonies, and were always carried out by priests. In some of these ceremonies, the Aztecs performed human sacrifices on an unparalleled scale. One report states that after one especially energetic military campaign, 20,000 captives were sacrificed.

Human sacrifice was most commonly found in the major public ceremonies. Often these ceremonies were accompanied by fasting; some food was prepared but it was made without chile or salt. Singing, dancing, mock combats, feasting, and other colorful events were also frequently included in ceremonies.

The Aztecs also practiced cannibalism in some religious ceremonies, in a fashion strictly controlled by certain rules. For example, only enemy captives were eaten and only their legs and arms could be consumed. No captor could partake of his own captive because a kind of kinship was always established between captor and captive. According to Sahagún, when a prisoner was taken the captor stated, "He is as my beloved son." And the captive replied, "He is as my beloved father." When a captor then offered his captive to the priests in the temple, he remarked, "Shall I, then, eat my own flesh?" The flesh was distributed to the warrior's relatives and cooked in a stew before being eaten.

Anthropologists and historians have searched for explanations of the Aztec customs of sacrifice and cannibalism. Some have suggested that cannibalism was important for dietary reasons, but this is unlikely because the central Mexican diet was normally adequate and varied. Others have suggested that sacrifice may have served to control population size, at least temporarily, in recently conquered provinces. This practice may also have made it easier for the Aztecs to administer conquered provinces, for a short time, because so many defeated warriors were taken off to be sacrificed.

In addition to the large sacrificial ceremonies, the Mexica also performed monthly ceremonies to commemorate a

A ceremonial knife used by priests in sacrificial religious rites to cut out the heart of enemy captives or persons impersonating gods. The handle is inlaid with a mosaic of turquoise, mother-of-pearl, and malachite.

An image of the earth monster Tlaltecuhtli carved into a stone slab. According to Mexica beliefs, Tlaltecuhtli swallowed the sun in the evening and released it again in the morning. He also devoured the hearts and blood of persons sacrificed to the gods.

particular god. In one ceremony, young men and women held mock battles; in another, boys raced to be the first to climb a pole and retrieve a sacred image; in yet another, children were lifted by the neck to help their growth. At several ceremonies, valiant warriors were presented with rewards, and sometimes nobles offered feasts to commoners.

Many rituals, however, took place in individual households. Most of these involved divination or curing. Although the Mexica were strongly fatalistic, believing that events were fixed in advance, they also felt they could try to influence their destiny. Individuals burdened with a bad day sign could carefully follow the exemplary life and counteract the negative effects of an unfortunate sign. Astrologers were always consulted to advise on favorable days for major events, from the planting of crops to the installation of a new ruler.

Divination was also used to solve daily problems and for curing illnesses. For this work, *shamans* were sometimes consulted. These were part-time religious specialists skilled in divination and curing. Shamans could be consulted to discover the identity of a thief or the cause or course of an illness. They diagnosed an illness by, for example, "reading" the distribution of maize kernels and beans thrown on a cloak or by knotting a cord and yanking it. (If the cord came untied, the patient would recover.) Some illnesses were believed to have been caused by supernatural

Carved wooden drum used for religious ceremonies and entertainment. Drums were usually accompanied by flutes and conch shells.

forces. Such cases required special cures. People wishing to become shamans were trained by experienced shamans.

In a world controlled by fate and uncertainty, the Mexica believed that certain omens could reveal their destiny. At night one might run into the apparitions of the fearsome "night axe" or the "bundle of ashes," the god Tezcatlipoca in his guise as a wizard. Many omens were tied to the animal world. For example, if a weasel crossed one's path, serious trouble was on its way. If a rabbit came into one's house, the house would be destroyed or the residents would run off like rabbits. If a skunk entered a house, death was not far away.

Starting about 10 years before the arrival of the Spaniards in 1519, ominous omens of an unusual type began to haunt the Mexica. A huge flame appeared each night for a year. Lightning struck the temple dedicated to the fire god. The waters of Lake Texcoco suddenly became violent for no apparent reason. In addition, a wailing woman appeared at night crying "O my beloved sons, now we are about to go!" These omens warned of a major, shocking event to come. ▲

Libro duodecimo

motcucalhuijque, njman
aoac maquijs. Auh in monte
mjctico, njman ieic callacq
val motzatzacutivezque.
Auh in in muchiuh ietla
qualizpan: auh in ieiuhquj
njmã ieic teiximacho, te
çaçaco: auh in iemuchintin
oçacoque in motcucalhuijq
njmã ieic tatlatilo in tetel
puchcali.

I njc cempoalli vmei Capitulo
vncan mjtoa in querjn Motecu
çoma, yoan ce vei pilli tlatelul
co mjcque: auh min nacaio quj
vallazque iquijia oaiuci quj ia
oaioc incalli in vncan catca
Sspañoles.

Capitulo. 23. de como Mokecuço
ma y el gouernador del Hatilulco
fueron echados muertos fuera de
la casa donde los españoles estaua
fortalecidos.

Despues delo arriba dicho, quatrodius
andados despues delamatança que
se hizo conel cu, hallaron los mexicanos
muertos a Motecucoma, y al gouer
nador del Hatilulco echados fuera de
delas casas reales cerca del muro dõ
de estaua vnapiedra labrada como
gala pago que llamaua Teoayoc: y
despues que conocieron los que los

Auh ie iuh navilhuijtl ne
tencalhuijloc in qujmontla
çaco in Motcuçoma, yoan
Jzquauhtzin, o mjcque, atl
co itaisian, Teoaioc: ca
vncan catca in jxiptla aioh,
tatl in tlaxiximtli, iuh qujn
aioh ipan mjxcuhtica in
tatl. Auh ino ittvque, ino i

The first page of chapter 23 in book 12 of Sahagún's Historia
General de las Cosas de Nueva España. *The illustration shows
the Spaniards casting Motecuhzoma and a nobleman from a palace
after their death in Tenochtitlan.*

THE
SPANISH
CONQUEST

For almost 10 years, Motecuhzoma's astrologers tried earnestly to interpret the omens that the people had been observing, but they were unable to agree on their meaning. Meanwhile, some old men and women had reported having disturbing dreams. According to Friar Durán, one old man told Motecuhzoma that

> these last nights the Lords of Sleep have shown us the temple of Huitzilopochtli burning with frightful flames, the stones falling one by one until it was totally destroyed. We also saw Huitzilopochtli himself fallen, cast down upon the floor! This is what we have dreamed!

The old women saw "the great chieftains and lords filled with fright, abandoning the city and fleeing toward the hills." Astrologers from several nearby cities, including Texcoco, feared that the dreams predicted some unimaginable disaster. Now nervous, Motecuhzoma challenged the ruler of Texcoco to a ball game to determine the truth of these predictions. Motecuhzoma lost, which signified that the prediction of imminent disaster was correct.

Soon after the game, messengers arrived from the coast with distressing news that strange "mounds" had appeared on the ocean. The year was probably Thirteen Rabbit, or 1518. Motecuhzoma wondered whether the appearance of the mounds signaled the coming of Quetzalcoatl. According to Mexica mythologies, the god had left Mexico several centuries earlier, vowing to return and reclaim his kingdom in the year One Reed.

Hernando Cortés arrived on the east coast of Mexico in 1519. On the Aztec calendar, it was the year One Reed. With visions of gaining riches, Cortés had sailed from Cuba, where he had been for about 7 years, to Mexico with about 600 men and 16 horses, in 11 ships. The first encounters with the coastal Indians were disastrous for the Spaniards; they ended in full-scale battles. However, when Cortés and his men put ashore on the coast near the site of the present-day city of Veracruz, they were met by ambassadors from Motecuhzoma. These men brought

An old man's dream that the Mexica temples were burning just prior to the arrival of Hernando Cortés. A burning temple was the symbol of conquest. (From the Florentine Codex*)*

with them expensive gifts and the attire of Quetzalcoatl, which included a sleeveless jacket, turquoise mosaic serpent mask, greenstone earplugs and necklace, obsidian sandals, and a mirror for his back. They climbed aboard Cortés's ship, where they insisted on dressing the Spanish leader in the god's array because they believed he was Quetzalcoatl, returning as promised in the year One Reed. Cortés allowed himself to be dressed and then responded by firing a cannon, a completely novel and unnerving experience for the royal ambassadors.

The Spaniards spent about five months on the coast. By the time they began to move inland toward Tenochtitlan, Motecuhzoma had decided to await their inevitable arrival. At first he was uncertain as to whether the Span-

iards were gods or humans. However, he decided to send out several envoys, including sorcerers, to try to discourage Cortés and his troops from making the journey to Tenochtitlan.

The Spaniards marched inland, fighting local people at times as they went. Cortés met enemies of the great Motecuhzoma, and he convinced them to join him in his move on Tenochtitlan. The most powerful of these were the Tlaxcallans, who fought the Spaniards to a standstill. Finally the two sides arrived at a peaceful agreement: The Tlaxcallans would join the Spaniards in their attempt to defeat Motecuhzoma. Cortés continued his march on Tenochtitlan with about 350 Spaniards (some

The Spaniards, under Hernando Cortés, arrive on the coast of Mexico. They brought with them horses, wheat, and other items that the people of Mexico had never seen. (From the Florentine Codex*)*

had stayed in Veracruz, others had died) and several thousand Tlaxcallans.

During the march, Motecuhzoma's messengers greeted Cortés on several occasions, sometimes with gifts, other times with sorcery or blockades to discourage him. But Cortés would not be discouraged or sidetracked, and in early November the Mexica and Spanish leaders finally met face to face. Motecuhzoma welcomed the Spaniards and their Tlaxcallan allies into the city.

Cortés and his men became Motecuhzoma's guests in Tenochtitlan. Even though they were guests in a strange city and greatly outnumbered, the Spaniards had their goals of conquest firmly in mind. They were especially eager to acquire gold and other treasure and were intent on converting the people to Christianity. While living as guests in a royal palace, Cortés's men found a magnificent treasure room, which they plundered. When Motecuhzoma took Cortés on a tour of the city and they were atop the great temple, Cortés shocked the watching Mexica when he ordered his troops to throw the figures representing gods down the temple steps.

Perhaps convinced by the omens of evil, Motecuhzoma had apparently concluded that the newcomers would be triumphant. He did not resist, even when Cortés, soon after arriving, took the Mexica ruler prisoner in his own city.

Meanwhile, the Cuban governor, Diego Velasquez, had sent more Spanish ships to arrest Cortés. Cortés had

Hernando Cortés was described by his chaplain, Francisco López de Gómera, as "rowdy, mischievous and wayward, a lover of arms." This portrait, which hangs in a hospital founded by Cortés in Mexico City, was painted more than a century after Cortés's death.

sailed to Mexico without authorization. When Cortés learned that Spanish ships had arrived in Veracruz, he and some of his men left Tenochtitlan to meet them. Using promises of great riches, Cortés convinced the 900 new arrivals to join him. He returned to Tenochtitlan with his new forces only to find the men he had left there trapped and under attack. In the subsequent fighting, Motecuhzoma was killed. With their important hostage dead and their supplies dwindling, the Spaniards decided to flee the city and try to return later. They attempted to leave on a drizzly night in July 1520, a night that would come to be known as the Noche Triste, or "Sorrowful Night."

The Mexica army intercepted their flight. Spaniards, with their Tlaxcallan allies, fought the Mexica face-to-face all night. The losses were extremely heavy. The exact number of Mexica casualties is unknown. Cortés probably lost more than half his men, and as many as 2,000 to 3,000 Tlaxcallans fell in the battle. With only about 425 men and 23 horses, Cortés and his remaining Tlaxcallan warriors painfully marched back to Tlaxcalla, harassed by Mexica warriors every step of the way.

The Spaniards stayed in Tlaxcalla for almost six months, nursing their wounds, recruiting reinforcements (especially more Tlaxcallans), and planning their next step. Meanwhile Tenochtitlan, despite its initial victory, was weakening. Smallpox, which had been brought by the Europeans, had already claimed the life of Cuitlahuac (Kwee-TLA-wak), the ruler who followed Motecuhzoma. The disease began spreading through the city.

The next ruler, Cuauhtemoc (Kwauh-TE-mok), anticipating a determined attack from the Spaniards, worked hard to hold his lakeshore allies and bring supplies into the city. Cortés competed with Cuauhtemoc to befriend the same

On what came to be known as the Noche Triste *(Sorrowful Night), the Spaniards and their Tlaxcallan allies fled Tenochtitlan, pursued by Mexica warriors. Cortés was wounded in the flight. (From the Florentine Codex)*

people. In the end many of the Mexica's allies or conquered subjects decided to associate themselves with the Spaniards. Among the most powerful of these were the citizens of Texcoco, and at Texcoco, Cortés spent much time constructing ships to attack the island city.

Cortés began his formal attack on the capital of the Aztec Empire on April 28, 1521. He had more than 900 Spaniards, thousands of Indian allies, 86 horses, 15 cannons, and 13 ships. Cortés used his ships to blockade and attack Tenochtitlan. The Mexica had placed large stakes in the lake and stopped several of Cortés's ships. Cortés then marched his men into the city along the causeways. The street fighting was ferocious, costly, and exhausting. The Mexica and their allies killed many of the enemy and captured about 50 Spaniards, whom they sacrificed to Huitzilopochtli.

Cortés soon realized that he could not defeat the city by direct attack and decided instead to blockade the city and cut off its supplies. Witnesses reported to Sahagún that for a month and a half in the summer of 1521

> there was hunger. Many died of famine. There was no more good, pure water to drink—only nitrous water. Many died of it—contracted dysentery which killed them. The people ate anything—lizards, barn swallows, corn leaves, saltgrass; they gnawed . . . leather and buckskin, cooked or toasted; or sedum and adobe bricks. Never had such suffering been seen; it was terrifying how many of us died when we were shut in as we were.

In mid-July the Spaniards again attacked the weakened city. On August 13 they captured the ruler Cuauhtemoc. The Mexica were finally defeated. The siege had lasted 75 days. Cortés had been in Mexico for about two and a half years.

Considering what the Spaniards had to overcome, their success is remarkable. They were a small group of men with few supplies, fighting in a strange land populated by several million people. There were three important reasons for their success: superior weapons, effective military tactics, and the loose political structure of their opponents.

The Aztecs fought with lances, bows and arrows, and clubs tipped with sharp obsidian blades. For protection they held wooden shields and wore dense, tightly quilted cotton armor. The Spaniards, in contrast, wielded steel swords, fired muskets and cannons, and held steel shields for protection. The swords were especially effective in hand-to-hand combat. The guns and cannons offered shock value, but ultimately they were awkward and did little damage because of the time needed to reload. The horses and large dogs brought by the Spaniards also were strategic advantages, primarily

The Spaniards and their Indian allies use ships to make their final attack on the island city of Tenochtitlan, capital of the Aztec Empire. (From the Florentine Codex)

During Cortés's final attack on Tenochtitlan, some Spaniards were captured and then sacrificed. Their heads and those of their horses were displayed as trophies. (From the Florentine Codex)

because they startled the Indians, who had never seen such animals before.

The Spaniards' military strategies were also in their favor. The Aztecs, as was their custom, took daring chances in battle to try to capture their enemies for sacrifice. The Spaniards fought to defeat rather than capture. In hand-to-hand combat, therefore, they struck to kill. Also, the Aztecs usually brought only a small part of their forces to bear against an enemy at any one time. They did not throw all their warriors on the field to overwhelm an outnumbered enemy. The Spaniards, however, were able to amass a vast force. They almost always had Indian allies with them: Tlaxcallan warriors who had never been defeated by the Aztecs and many of the

Mexica's old allies and subjects. Because of the loose organization of their empire, the Mexica had only a weak hold on their allies and conquered subjects. These people were often very willing to rebel and aid the Spaniards.

While two great armies fought each other on the battlefields, the real conflict was between two civilizations, Indian and European. When the siege ended, the Spaniards had not only conquered a great city but were also about to change an entire civilization. For the Indians, the end of this war meant more than a change in rulers and a shifting of tribute duties. The new lords of the land ruled in a way that was different from that of any Indian conquerors before them. The Spaniards brought with them many new ideas, goals, laws, and material goods that were to transform the lives of the Mexica, Tlaxcallans, and all other Mexican Indians.

The first change had already begun to occur almost immediately after the Spaniards arrived in Mexico. The Indian population started to decline. Warfare was one cause, but the major cause was the introduction of European diseases such as smallpox and measles. The Indians had no immunity to these diseases, which quickly generated deadly epidemics. The tlatoani Cuitlahuac caught smallpox and died just six months after he came to power, even before the Spaniards laid siege to Tenochtitlan. Repeatedly, massive epidemics hit the Indians throughout the rest of the 16th century, and by 1570 the Indian population was probably only

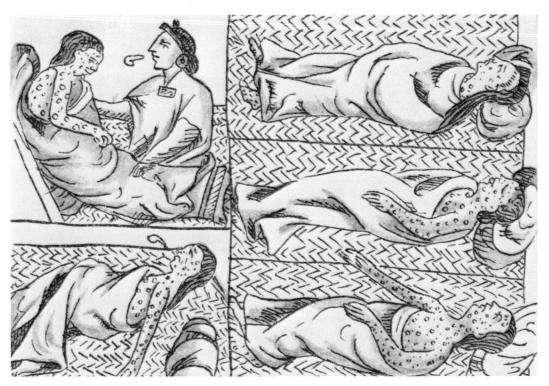

Even before Tenochtitlan fell to the Spaniards, smallpox swept through the city. The disease, to which the Indians had no immunity, devastated the Indian population in the 16th century. (From the Florentine Codex)

one-third to one-half of its preconquest size.

The Mexica population changed in another way when Spanish conquerors began to marry Indian women and have children, even as the conquest was in progress. These children were called *mestizo* (of mixed Spanish-Indian parentage). The intermarrying process was not, however, just a mixing of genetic heritage but, more important, a blending of cultural heritage. As the centuries passed, Spaniard married Indian, mestizo married mestizo, Spaniard married mestizo, and Indian married mestizo.

By 1821, when Spanish rule in Mexico finally came to an end, probably one-third of the population was mestizo.

Indians and Spaniards had different material goods. Both the introduction of new Spanish products and the decline in use of certain Indian goods brought change to the Aztec culture. The Spaniards introduced metal tools (including machetes and plows), the wheel, carts and wagons, and hardy draft animals. Cattle, horses, sheep, goats, pigs, donkeys, mules, and chickens also arrived with the newcomers. They also brought new crops, such as

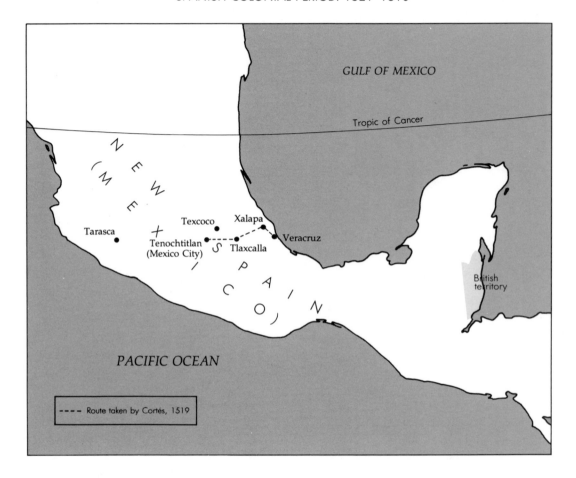

GULF OF MEXICO

Tropic of Cancer

NEW (M)EX(W)EX(I)C(O)

S(P)A(I)N

Tarasca

Texcoco

Xalapa

Tenochtitlan
(Mexico City)

Tlaxcalla

Veracruz

British territory

PACIFIC OCEAN

- - - - Route taken by Cortés, 1519

wheat and sugarcane as well as olives, grapes, and various other fruits.

The Indians, in turn, introduced the Spaniards to many new items, especially such popular foods as maize, tomatoes, and chocolate. They also had the work of their specialized artisans to show, such as elegant feather fans and gold lip plugs. But now the artisans had few wealthy nobles or Spaniards as customers for these items. Their craft production did not continue for long after the conquest. Carpenters, potters, and canoe makers, however, who produced practical goods instead of luxuries, were in great demand. Many Indians in these occupations or those who had other useful skills were kept busy during the three centuries of Spanish rule. Others learned new crafts, such as Spanish-style tailoring.

The work patterns of the Indians changed in other ways. One reason was the Spaniards' great interest in acquiring gold and silver. The conquerors established large mines, and many

Indians found their daily life changed dramatically as they worked in these mines under difficult conditions.

Under Spanish control, a major change in Aztec society occurred as the 16th century continued. The divisions between Aztec nobles and commoners became increasingly vague. There were new ways for commoners to acquire wealth. Also, the Spaniards changed the Aztecs' governmental structure. A multilevel system of government was put in place by the king of Spain and the positions of colonial authority were filled by Spaniards. Indian nobles no longer ran the government, although for a while they did run local town councils. Still, they could make deci-

sions only with the approval of the Spanish authorities. Some local Indian rulers became local governors under the Spanish administration. Through contact with the Spaniards in the colonial period, these and many other Indian nobles rapidly went through a process of *acculturation*; they changed their own ways, learning those of the dominant Spanish culture. These people still had enough of their former wealth to buy Spanish clothing and furniture and had avenues to provide a Spanish-style education for their children. Into the late 16th century, some nobles managed to hold on to some of their old rights and wealth. However, they were still below the Spaniards on the social ladder.

A 17th-century view of Mexico City, formerly Tenochtitlan. This engraving is captioned in French and the marketplace of Tlatelolco is marked in the center. The Spaniards destroyed many of the major Aztec buildings during and shortly after their conquest.

An outdoor market in Xicotepec, in eastern central Mexico. Mexican markets today are still a place where people gather to share information and buy housewares and clothing, much of it handcrafted, and food.

At the same time, many commoners were climbing the social ladder by becoming enterprising businessmen and acquiring wealth. For example, in Tlaxcalla, cochineal (a bright red dye from an insect) became a prized item for the Spanish markets in Mexico and Europe. Records indicate that some commoners became skilled at large-scale production of this dye. The old Tlaxcallan nobles were outraged as well as nervous when they saw commoners gaining wealth and importance in the eyes of the Spanish overlords.

While the Indians were growing wheat alongside maize, and nobles and commoners were merging into a single social class, religious beliefs and practices were also changing. The Christian Spaniards felt that it was their mission to convert other peoples and save their souls. Soon after the conquest, friars arrived in Mexico. The Catholic friars combined religious teachings with other types of education and established schools in their monasteries. Aztec children, mostly those of nobles, attended these schools. They learned reading, writing, mathematics, singing, and how to play musical instruments. The friars' primary goal was still to stamp out the native gods and replace them with the Christian god.

The friars were confronted with a major problem. Whereas Christianity was a religion that rejected foreign gods, the Aztec religion had traditionally absorbed them. Therefore, it was not unusual for the Indians to accept the Christian god as another one of many in their pantheon. This was not what the friars had intended. A long, painful religious conflict ensued. Over the years, the Indians came to identify some Christian saints with some of their traditional gods. Even today, in some Indian villages Aztec gods are linked to Catholic saints. For example, the adored Virgin of Guadalupe reflects a blend of beliefs about the Aztec mother goddess Tonantzin and the Catholic Virgin Mary.

The Aztecs did not always welcome or willingly accept changes. Both nobles and commoners often firmly resisted many of the Spanish ways. Motecuhzoma's poets and philosophers found it difficult to accept the loss of their great and powerful civilization. In disbelief they saw the end of their world and asked, "Who could conquer Tenochtitlan? Who could shake the foundation of heaven?"

The foundation of heaven had been shaken, but it had not been destroyed. Although the Aztec Empire as it was in the early 16th century has long since passed away, thousands of Aztec descendants still live in Mexico today. Many of these people speak Spanish, purchase prepared food in stores, and wear store-bought clothing. However, they still carry aspects of the ancient Aztec culture with them, from their language to their ways of preparing food to weaving on the ancient-style loom. Mexican Spanish is sprinkled with worlds of Nahuatl origin, some of

An Indian woman peels tomatillos at the open-air market at Xicotepec.

which, especially those for foods — tomato, chile, tamale — have entered English and other languages as well. Artisans still produce traditional pottery, mats, and cloth. At the well-ordered marketplaces some people still sell small amounts of their produce and crafts and barter for other goods. And as more artifacts are retrieved and historical documents are translated, archaeologists have a chance to dig a little deeper into the past, to glimpse the power and glory of the center of the Aztec Empire, Tenochtitlan. ▲

BIBLIOGRAPHY

Anderson, Arthur J. O., and Charles Dibble, eds. and trans. *The War of Conquest: How It Was Waged Here in Mexico*. Salt Lake City: University of Utah Press, 1978.

Anonymous Conqueror. "Relación de algunas cosas de la Nueva España y de la Gran Ciudad de Temestitan México." In *Colección de Documentos para la Historia de México*, vol. 1. Edited by J. C. Icazbalceta. México: Editorial Porrua, 1971.

Berdan, Frances F. *The Aztecs of Central Mexico: An Imperial Society*. New York: Holt, Rinehart & Winston, 1982.

Bray, Warwick. *Everyday Life of the Aztecs*. New York: Dorset Press, 1968.

Davies, Nigel. *The Aztecs*. New York: Putnam, 1974.

Díaz del Castillo, Bernal. *The Discovery and Conquest of Mexico*. Translated by A. P. Maudslay. New York: Noonday, 1956.

————. *The Conquest of New Spain*. Baltimore: Penguin, 1963.

Durán, Diego. *The Aztecs: The History of the Indies of New Spain*. Translated by Doris Heyden and Fernando Horcasitas. New York: Orion, 1964.

————. *Book of the Gods and Rites and The Ancient Calendar*. Translated by Doris Heyden and Fernando Horcasitas. Norman: University of Oklahoma Press, 1971.

Fagan, Brian M. *The Aztecs*. New York: Freeman, 1984.

León-Portilla, Miguel. *Pre-Columbian Literatures of Mexico*. Norman: University of Oklahoma Press, 1969.

————. "The Ethnohistorical Record for the Huey Teocalli of Tenochtitlan." In *The Aztec Templo Mayor*. Edited by Elizabeth Boone. Washington, DC: Dumbarton Oaks Research Library and Collection, 1987.

Lewis, Oscar. *Tepoztlan: Life in Mexico*. New York: Holt, Rinehart & Winston, 1960.

McDowell, Bart. "The Aztecs." *National Geographic* 158, no. 6 (December 1980): 704–751.

Motolinia, Toribio. "History of the Indians of New Spain." In *Documents and Narratives Concerning the Discovery and Conquest of Latin America*, New Series no. 4. Edited by Elizabeth Foster. Berkeley: The Cortés Society, 1950.

Sahagún, Bernardino de. *Florentine Codex: General History of the Things of New Spain*. Translated by Arthur J. O. Anderson and Charles Dibble. Salt Lake City and Santa Fe: University of Utah Press and School of American Research, 1950–1982.

Soustelle, Jacques. *Daily Life of the Aztecs on the Eve of the Spanish Conquest*. Stanford: Stanford University Press, 1970.

Zorita, Alonso de. *Life and Labor in Ancient Mexico*. Translated by Benjamin Keen. New Brunswick, N.J.: Rutgers University Press, 1963.

THE AZTECS AT A GLANCE

TRIBE *Mexica (The word* Aztec *refers to all peoples of central Mexico who were part of the Triple Alliance, or Aztec, Empire.)*

CULTURE AREA *Mesoamerica*

GEOGRAPHY *Valley of Mexico*

LINGUISTIC FAMILY *Uto-Aztecan (Nahuatl)*

CAPITAL CITY *Tenochtitlan*

POPULATION *capital city 150,000–200,000 (est.)*
Valley of Mexico 1,000,000 (est.)

EMPIRE FLOURISHED *1430–1519*

FIRST EUROPEAN CONTACT *Hernando Cortés, Spanish, 1519*

GLOSSARY

acculturation The process by which one culture changes and adapts to the dominant culture it confronts.

amantecatl (a-man-Te-kahtl) (pl. *amantecah*) Professional artisans who made luxury items of feathers for the nobility and occupied an intermediate position in the Mexica class system.

archaeology The systematic recovery and study of evidence of human ways of life, especially of prehistoric peoples.

atolli (a-TO-lee) A dish of maize gruel typically eaten by commoners.

Aztec The general term for the civilization of several Indian groups of central Mexico that had similar languages and shared customs during the two centuries before the Spanish conquest. One of these groups, the Mexica, is popularly known as the Aztecs.

cacao A tropical tree whose seedpods contain seeds, or beans, that are processed to produce chocolate. Cacao beans were used as currency in the Aztec Empire.

cacahuatl (ka-KA-watl) A hot chocolate drink that was a luxury item for the Mexica.

calmecac (kal-ME-kak) A school run by priests and attended by noble boys once they reached age 15.

calpulli (kal-PO-lee) A district within a town or city having its own local government, patron god, school, and lands.

Chichimeca (chee-chee-ME-ka) Nomadic hunting and gathering tribes of the northern desert regions of Mexico. The Mexica were one of these groups.

chinampas (chee-NAM-paz) Plots of land built in shallow lakebeds by alternating layers of vegetation and mud; used to increase available residential and agricultural land.

city-state An autonomous political unit consisting of one major urban center and the smaller communities in the surrounding area.

codex (pl. *codices*) A handwritten book; an official record or report written in hieroglyphics (picture symbols) by a scribe.

cuicacalli (kwee-ka-KA-lee) A school where children ages 12 to 15 learned how to sing, dance, and play musical instruments.

divination Attempts to obtain knowledge of unknown present or future events or to discover identities of people or causes of illnesses.

ethnography The systematic observation and description of the variety of human cultures or ways of life.

glyph A drawn symbol in a writing system that stands for a word, idea, sound, or syllable.

guild An organization of artisans or merchants; members lived in their own communities and trained novices.

Huitzilopochtli (wee-tsee-lo-POCH-tlee) The patron god of the Mexica and a war god to whom warriors dedicated their service; also, in some myths, a sun god.

macehaulli (ma-se-WAL-lee) (pl. *macehualtin*) A free commoner who worked at farming, fishing, or crafts and was trained to serve in the army.

mayeque (ma-YE-kay) A landless peasant who worked on lands owned by nobles. Mayeque were not members of a calpulli.

mestizo A person of mixed Indian-Spanish ancestry.

Mexica (me-SHEE-ka) The name the Aztecs called themselves; the Chichimec group that founded Tenochtitlan and later became the dominant partner of the Triple Alliance, or Aztec, Empire.

Mictlan (MEEK-tlan) The underworld of eternal darkness and emptiness where most people descended when they died, according to Mexica beliefs.

Nahuatl (NA-watl) The Aztec language.

patolli (pah-TO-lee) A board game played with markers and dice.

pochtecatl (poch-TE-katl) (pl. *pochtecah*) A professional merchant who occupied an intermediate position in the Mexica class system.

polygyny A form of marriage in which a man has two or more wives at one time. In Aztec society, polygyny was a privilege practiced by nobles.

pulque An alcoholic drink made from the fermented juices of the root of the maguey plant.

Quetzalcoatl (ket-tsal-KO-atl) A creator god credited with having given arts and maize to humans; also known as the feathered serpent and the morning star.

shaman A practitioner who calls on supernatural powers to solve problems, heal the sick, or ensure success in acquiring food or other essential activities.

tamale A dish made from ground corn dough filled with various ingredients and baked inside corn husks; a typical food of the Mexica.

tecutli (te-KUT-tlee) (pl. *tetecutlin*) A noble chief of high rank in the Mexica class system; often served as an adviser to a ruler or as a judge, general, or tax collector.

telpochcalli (tel-poch-KA-lee) A district school that provided formal education to commoner boys starting when they reached age 15.

Tenochtitlan (te-noch-TEET-lan) The capital city founded by the Mexica in 1325, on an island in Lake Texcoco; within present-day Mexico City.

Tezcatlipoca (tes-kat-lee-PO-ka) A major sun god; patron of young warriors.

tianquiztli (tee-an-KEES-tlee) The central Mexica marketplace where members of a community gathered to trade goods and services.

tlachtli (TLACH-tlee) A ball game played on an *I*-shaped court in which players tried to hit a rubber ball through one of two rings along the center walls of the court.

tlacotli (tla-KOT-tlee) (pl. *tlacotin*) A slave who owed his labor, but not his personal freedom, to another. People could become slaves by committing a crime or being sold by themselves or their parents.

Tlaloc (TLA-lok) The Mexica god of rain and fertility.

Tlatelolco (tla-te-LOL-ko) The sister-city of Tenochtitlan; site of the largest marketplace in the Mexica settlement.

tlatoani (tla-to-A-nee) (pl. *tlatoque*) The noble ruler of a region, city-state, or town. This position was the highest in the Mexica class system.

toltecatl (tol-TE-katl) (pl. *toltecah*) An artisan who crafted fine luxury items for the nobles and who occupied an intermediate position in the Mexica class system.

tonalamatl (to-na-LA-matl) The guide used by astrologers to predict a child's fate.

tonalpohualli (to-nal-po-WHA-lee) The Mexica ritual 260-day calendar made up of 20 name days and the numbers 1 through 13; literally, "count of days."

Tonatiuh (to-na-TEE-yooh) The sun god who rules the current age and whose sun will eventually be destroyed by earthquakes, according to Mexica beliefs.

tribute Goods and wealth collected by a powerful state from its conquered subjects.

Triple Alliance The military alliance of the cities of Tenochtitlan, Texcoco, and Tlacopan in the 15th century to create the Aztec Empire.

INDEX

PICTURE CREDITS

From plate 51 of *Aztec Art* by Esther Pasztory, published by Harry N. Abrams, Inc., 1983, p. 86; Dr. Frances Berdan, pp. 17, 102, 103; The Bettmann Archive, pp. 22, 26, 30, 95, 101; The Bodleian Library, Oxford University, Codex Mendoza, MS. Arch Seld. A.1, fol 69r, p. 12; 2r, p. 24; 46r, p. 34; 64r, p. 36; 67r, p. 48; 68r, p. 56; 60r, p. 62; 70r, pp. 73, 75; Lee Boltin, p. 67 *top and bottom right*; Lee Boltin/British Museum, pp. 68–69; courtesy of the Brooklyn Museum, pp. 43, 52; Hillel Burger/Peabody Museum, Harvard University, p. 74; courtesy of the Department of Library Services, American Museum of Natural History, pp. 14, 19, 31, 40, 59, 78, 80 *right*, 84, 89, 90, 98; Dumbarton Oaks Research Library and Collections, Washington, D.C., pp. 68 *bottom*, 82; Kenneth Garrett/Woodfin Camp, pp. 65, 66–67; Giraudon/Art Resource, p. 27; Carmelo Guadagno/Museum of the American Indian, Heye Foundation, p. 88 *left*; The Metropolitan Museum of Art, New York, gift of Frederick E. Church, 1983, p. 28; The Metropolitan Museum of Art, New York, purchase, 1900, p. 83 *left*; Museo Nacional de Antropología, Mexico City/Giraudon/Art Resource, p. 83 *right*; Museo Nacional de Antropología, Mexico City/photo: National Gallery of Art, Washington, D.C., pp., 51, 68 *top*; Museo Nacional de Antropología, Mexico City/SEF/Art Resource, p. 87; Lesley Newhart, pp. 15, 29; Peabody Museum, Harvard University, pp. 70–71; Photoreporters, Inc., p. 42; Proyecto Templo Mayor/National Gallery of Art, Washington, D.C., p. 72; Andrew Rakoczy/Bruce Coleman Inc., p. 67 *bottom left*; Scala/Art Resource, pp. 44, 60, 88 *right*; SEF/Art Resource, p. 53; The Time Museum, Rockford, Illinois, p. 80 *left*; University of Utah Press, Salt Lake City, pp. 18, 38, 39, 45, 46, 50, 64, 92, 94, 96, 97, 99; Norman Weiser/British Museum, cover.

Maps (pp. 2, 33, 100) by Gary Tong.

FRANCES F. BERDAN is professor of anthropology and chair of the anthropology department at California State University, San Bernardino. She received her B.A. in geography from Michigan State University and her Ph.D. in anthropology from the University of Texas at Austin. She has done ethnographic research in Mexico, archaeological work in New Mexico, and archival research in Spain and Mexico. She has written five books and numerous articles; the books include *The Aztecs of Central Mexico: An Imperial Society* (1982), *Beyond the Codices* (1976, with Arthur J. O. Anderson and James Lockhart), *The Tlaxcallan Actas* (1986, with James Lockhart and Arthur J. O. Anderson), *The Matrícula de Tributos* (1980, with Jacqueline de Durand-Forest), and *Spanish Thread on Indian Looms* (1988, with Russell J. Barber). Her current research concerns are traditional weaving and textiles in the Sierra Norte de Puebla, Mexico, the 16th-century Codex Mendoza, colonial Nahuatl census documents, and the economic and political structure of the Aztec Empire.

FRANK W. PORTER III, general editor of INDIANS OF NORTH AMERICA, is director of the Chelsea House Foundation for American Indian Studies. He holds a B.A., M.A., and Ph.D. from the University of Maryland. He has done extensive research concerning the Indians of Maryland and Delaware and is the author of numerous articles on their history, archaeology, geography, and ethnography. He was formerly director of the Maryland Commission on Indian Affairs and American Indian Research and Resource Institute, Gettysburg, Pennsylvania, and he has received grants from the Delaware Humanities Forum, the Maryland Committee for the Humanities, the Ford Foundation, and the National Endowment for the Humanities, among others. Dr. Porter is the author of *The Bureau of Indian Affairs* in the Chelsea House KNOW YOUR GOVERNMENT series.